GW00838448

M366 Block 3
UNDERGRADUATE COMPUTING

Natural and artificial intelligence

Natural intelligence

Block 3

Cover image: Daniel H. Janzen. *Polistes* wasps build a relatively simple nest that lasts only a single summer. These New World wasps often site the unenclosed combs under eaves and the other sheltered places where they come into contact with people.

This publication forms part of an Open University course M366 *Natural and artificial intelligence*. Details of this and other Open University courses can be obtained from the Student Registration and Enquiry Service, The Open University, PO Box 197,
Milton Keynes MK7 6BJ, United Kingdom: tel. +44 (0)845 300 6090, email general-enquiries@open.ac.uk

Alternatively, you may visit the Open University website at
http://www.open.ac.uk where you can learn more about the wide range of courses and packs offered at all levels by The Open University.

To purchase a selection of Open University course materials visit
http://www.ouw.co.uk, or contact Open University Worldwide, Michael Young Building, Walton Hall, Milton Keynes MK7 6AA, United Kingdom for a brochure.
tel. +44 (0)1908 858793; fax +44 (0)1908 858787; email ouw-customer-services@open.ac.uk

The Open University
Walton Hall, Milton Keynes
MK7 6AA

First published 2007, second edition 2008.

Edited, designed and typeset by The Open University.

Printed and bound in the United Kingdom by The Charlesworth Group, Wakefield.

ISBN 978 0 7492 5069 0

2.1

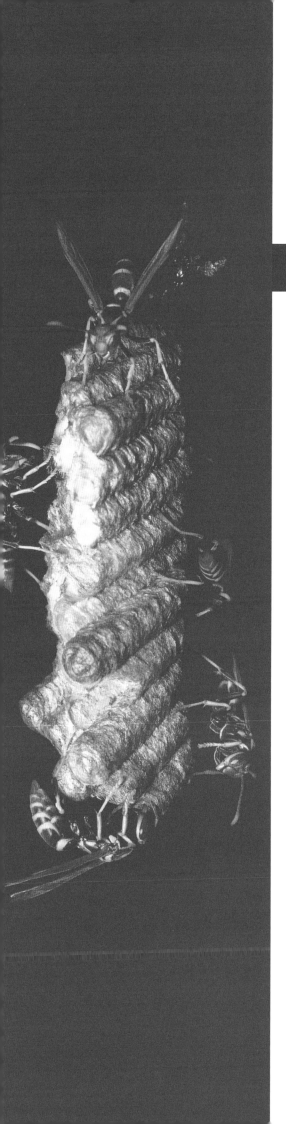

Block 3
Natural intelligence

Prepared for the course team by Chris Dobbyn and
Syed Mustafa Ali

CONTENTS

Introduction to Block 3		5
Unit 1:	Natural intelligence	9
Unit 2:	Mechanisms of natural intelligence	41
Unit 3:	Interaction and emergence in swarms	71
Unit 4:	Interaction, emergence, adaptation and selection in individuals	115
Conclusion to Block 3		165
References and further reading		167
Acknowledgements		169
Index for Block 3		170

M366 COURSE TEAM

Chair, author and academic editor
Chris Dobbyn

Authors
Mustafa Ali

Tony Hirst

Mike Richards

Neil Smith

Patrick Wong

External assessor
Nigel Crook, Oxford Brookes University

Course managers
Gaynor Arrowsmith

Linda Landsberg

Media development staff
Andrew Seddon, Media Project Manager

Garry Hammond, Editor

Kate Gentles, Freelance Editor

Callum Lester, Software Developer

Andrew Whitehead, Designer and Graphic Artist

Phillip Howe, Compositor

Sarah Gamman, Contracts Executive

Lydia Eaton, Media Assistant

Critical readers
Frances Chetwynd

John Dyke

Ian Kenny

Paolo Remagnino

Thanks are due to the Desktop Publishing Unit of the Faculty of Mathematics and Computing.

Introduction to Block 3

Block introduction

But now at last the sacred influence
Of light appears, and from the walls of Heav'n
Shoots farr into the bosom of dim Night
A glimmering dawn; here Nature first begins
Her fardest verge, and CHAOS to retire
As from her outmost works a brok'n foe
With tumult less and with less hostile din ...

Source: Milton, *Paradise Lost*, Book 2

Here hills and vales, the woodland and the plain,
Here earth and water, seem to strive again;
Not *Chaos* like together crush'd and bruis'd,
But as the world, harmoniously confus'd:
Where order in variety we see,
And where, tho' all things differ, all agree.

Source: Pope, *Windsor Forest*

In 1714, the philosopher and mathematician Gottfried Wilhelm Leibnitz wrote:

It is the knowledge of necessary and eternal truths which distinguishes us from mere animals, and gives us *Reason* and the sciences, raising us to knowledge of ourselves and of God. It is this in us which we call the rational soul or *Mind*.

Source: Leibnitz, *The Monadology*, sect. 29

This could almost be the motto of Block 2. There the argument runs like this: complex problems require intelligence to solve them, and intelligence is the domain of *humanity*, operating in the medium of knowledge, language and logic. Thus, all we have to do to understand the workings of our intelligence is to examine our own minds. Then, to create machine intelligence, the next step is to *represent* such knowledge and logical processes on a computer. A corollary of this argument has to be that creatures without language, logic and explicit knowledge – presumably most living things – are without intelligence. They are 'mere animals' whose behaviour is based on simple 'instinct'.

Our argument in this block, however, is that this is too narrow a view. The goal is to build intelligent machines. But by basing our understanding of intelligence simply on the contents of our own minds, as we perceive them, we may be making two serious mistakes:

▶ We may be failing to grasp ideas that could help us, ignoring powerful tools and techniques we could use on the problem.

▶ We are fixing only on activities which seem to require logical thought, and so could be severely limiting our idea of what intelligent behaviour actually *is*. Some behaviours might prove to be exceptionally difficult and complex, but require no explicit thought at all.

Unit 1: Natural intelligence

In Unit 1 we will try to develop a broader, more inclusive view of intelligence, one that looks beyond the human sphere, and which we call **natural intelligence**. You saw in Block 1, of course, that attempts to set up an all-purpose definition of 'intelligence' quickly run into sands of contradiction, ambiguity and doubt, so we will not attempt to repeat the exercise. We will simply try to open our eyes to some of the countless examples of ordered and purposeful behaviour that are to be found in the natural world, and consider what influence these might have on our understanding of 'intelligence'.

Unit 2: Mechanisms of natural intelligence

In Unit 2 we move on to look at four key mechanisms that seem to give rise to such behaviour: interaction, emergence, adaptation and selection. This is perhaps the most important unit of the course and develops the themes that will appear in every subsequent unit.

Unit 3: Interaction and emergence in swarms

Units 3 and 4 are more technical and develop important theoretical ideas. Unit 3 presents an extended discussion of how surprisingly sophisticated forms of intelligent behaviour can arise in swarms of simple agents, as a result of interaction and emergence, and how some of this behaviour can be replicated in computational systems to solve problems of optimisation, construction and analysis.

Unit 4: Interaction, emergence, adaptation and selection in individuals

Unit 4 deals with how the four principles can be harnessed in single agents as well – particularly robots, but also in systems that solve problems of optimisation and construction.

Although not specifically referred to in the text, you will find a variety of short video resources on the course DVD which illustrate insect, animal and robotic behaviour mentioned in the case studies.

Block 3 learning outcomes

After studying this block you will be able to:

▶ write a brief definition of the term 'natural intelligence';

▶ write a short paragraph defining the term 'nouvelle AI' and contrasting this with Symbolic AI;

▶ outline, and explain briefly, four principles that give rise to intelligent behaviour in the natural world;

▶ describe, with illustrative examples, some of the principles of ant colony optimisation and/or particle swarm optimisation, together with some of their potential applications;

▶ draw a set of explanatory diagrams demonstrating the principles of the subsumption architecture and potential fields methods;

▶ explain how adaptation and selection can be introduced into artificial intelligence systems.

Unit 1: Natural intelligence

CONTENTS

1	Introduction to Unit 1	10
	What you need to study this unit	10
	Learning outcomes for Unit 1	11
2	Preliminary examples	12
3	Natural intelligence	17
	3.1 Purposeful behaviour	18
	3.2 Systematic behaviour	21
	3.3 Structured and functional results	23
	3.4 Some conclusions	26
	3.5 A dreadful warning	30
	3.6 Natural, artificial, living	31
4	Natural and artificial intelligence	35
	4.1 Intelligence and knowledge	35
	4.2 Nouvelle AI	37
	4.3 A final caution	38
5	Summary of Unit 1	39
	References and further reading	167
	Acknowledgements	169
	Index for Block 3	170

Introduction to Unit 1

In this unit I will cast my net into the natural world by examining a number of short case studies, all based on observations of the behaviour of animals. I want to probe these for ideas that might help us to reconsider the rather narrow conception of intelligence we've been working with so far. I also want to challenge some commonly held ideas and distinctions. This is not a course on biology. But it *is* a course on how biology can inspire, change, improve and develop the computational techniques we need for truly intelligent computer systems.

What you need to study this unit

You will need the following course components, and will need to use your computer and internet connection for some of the exercises.

▶   this Block 3 text

▶   the course DVD.

LEARNING OUTCOMES FOR UNIT 1

After studying this unit you will be able to:

1.1 write a short paragraph outlining a broad definition of natural intelligence, rooted in some of the features of natural systems;

1.2 give a number of examples of natural systems that seem to be purposeful, systematic and ordered;

1.3 give contrasting definitions of the words 'natural', 'artificial' and 'living', explaining some of the difficulties that arise in drawing firm boundaries between them;

1.4 write a short definition of the term 'nouvelle AI' and contrast this with Symbolic AI.

2 Preliminary examples

The best way to start is by thinking about the following two case studies.

Case Study 1.1: Flocking and migrating birds

At one time or another, you will have witnessed the sight of a flock of birds, maybe hundreds strong, wheeling in the sky. Perhaps you didn't give it a second thought, but bird flocking does seem quite a mysterious phenomenon. The birds all keep formation, change course together, steer on the same heading. They seem to be moving as a single group, but there is no leader, no observable external guidance and no obvious way in which the birds might be communicating across the flock.

Even more striking is the phenomenon of migration. Most bird species migrate northwards in the spring to breed, and south in the winter to warmer climates where food will be plentiful.

Figure 1.1   Canada geese in flight

Some species travel by day, others by night; some fly in immense flocks, others alone. Many cover enormous distances: the arctic tern (*Sterna paradisaea*) migrates from Maine in the USA to the coast of Africa and then down to the Antarctic Circle, travelling as much as 35 000 kilometres a year. Most breeding and wintering grounds cover relatively small geographical areas, yet the birds find their way to them unerringly, year after year. For example, the greater snow goose (*Chen caerulescens atlantica*) breeds in a very specific region of the Canadian High Arctic, from the Foxe Basin to Alert on northern Ellesmere Island. They winter along the United States Atlantic coast, migrating more than 4000 kilometres, in flocks of between 35 and 1000 birds, depending on the season.

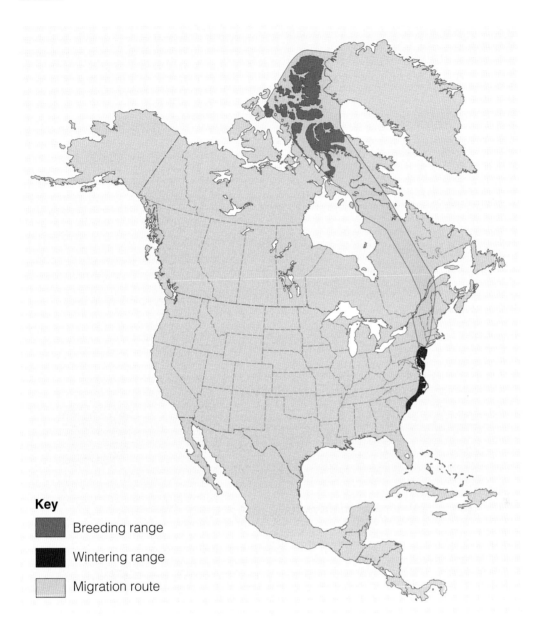

Key

Breeding range

Wintering range

Migration route

Figure 1.2   Snow goose migration routes

How birds are able to navigate with such accuracy is not fully understood, but most species are thought to use a number of range- and direction-finding strategies, including:

▶ steering by visual landmarks such as coastlines, rivers or mountains;

▶ setting flying courses by the sun (especially at sunset) and stars (especially the Pole Star and the constellations around it);

▶ following the Earth's magnetic field: iron-based minerals in birds' skulls enable them to fly north along magnetic field lines.

Some birds, such as petrels, also use their sense of smell to navigate, but only as a supplement to the mechanisms described above.

Case Study 1.2: Raiding army ants

The many species of carnivorous army ants (*Eciton*) live in colonies, maybe up to a million ants strong. Army ant nests are often referred to as 'bivouacs', because they are not earth constructions like those of other ant species – they are formed by the ants themselves, clustering together to form walls, fastening onto each other using their mandibles and claws on their legs. Despite being more or less blind, army ants search for prey in immense, highly organised groups – either swarms or columns, depending on the species. In a column raid, the ants spread out from the colony along a single trail from which foraging worker ants branch off along smaller columns. A swarm raid also starts along a trunk trail, which divides into numerous columns that then recombine into a single advancing swarm front.

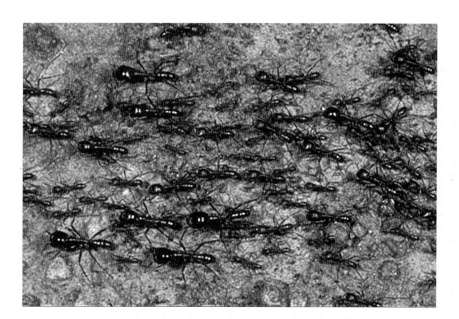

Figure 1.3   Army ants on the march

For regularity, organisation and sheer savagery, nothing quite matches the swarm raider (*E. burchelli*): a single colony may consume 100 000 prey items a day and bring back as many as 30 000 from a single raid. At dawn, pioneer ants set out, first along a base column connected to the bivouac and then fanning out in a complex network of columns along a swarm front up to 15 metres long and 2 metres deep. Individual ants move forward from the front and then retreat; and as each ant turns, another passes it, extending the front further.

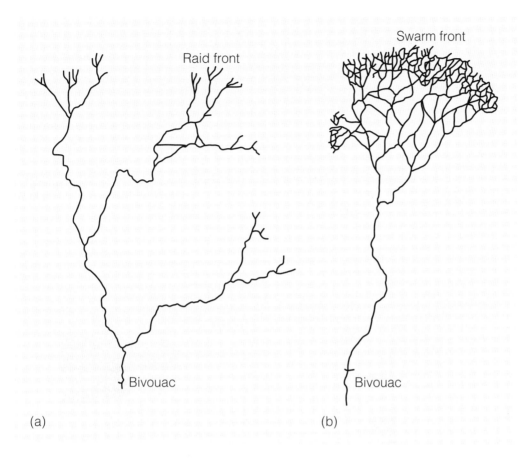

Figure 1.4   (a) Army ant column raid. (b) Swarm raid

Smaller insects, and even relatively huge creatures such as cockroaches, scorpions, grasshoppers and earthworms are flushed out, overwhelmed and stung to death by the advancing mass. Their corpses are sawn up and the pieces transported back to the colony by streams of workers along a labyrinth of trails behind the main front. Unbelievably, army ants have been observed to kill and dismember chickens, goats and even pigs, if the animals have previously been injured and are already helpless.

SAQ 1.1

From your own general knowledge, try to think of one or two other examples of similar behaviour to that described in the above case studies.

ANSWER...

One doesn't have to be a zoologist to know that examples abound. Birds and termites build complicated nests. Whales and bees carry out remarkable feats of navigation and communication. Fish and mammals such as wildebeest travel and defend each other in apparently organised schools or herds.

Exercise 1.1

What seems significant about behaviours like these, as compared to some other natural process, such as an avalanche, the flow of a river, the piling up of rocks by a glacier, etc? Note down some general characteristics that both the above case studies seem to have in common.

Discussion ....

Obviously there are key differences between the behaviour of an ant swarm, say, and an avalanche or any other purely physical phenomenon. First, the swarm seems to be *purposeful* – all that activity is unmistakably directed towards a clear end, the feeding of the colony. The same is true of the movement of birds. This certainly can't be said of avalanches, rivers, and so on: their actions seem to be governed by chance and the results are haphazard. Second, the behaviour of the animals in the case studies looks *systematic*. At first glance, an ant raid might look like a boiling confusion but, as we have seen, it follows a very regular pattern; so too do the flight patterns of the birds. Such activity can lead to complex and *structured* results, such as the elaborate nests of termites or birds.

There can be no argument that the natural world is full of such purpose and order. But purpose and order are surely two characteristics we might associate with intelligent behaviour.

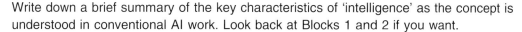 3 Natural intelligence

Before we go on, we should perhaps remind ourselves of the view of 'intelligence' we took in Block 2.

Exercise 1.2

Write down a brief summary of the key characteristics of 'intelligence' as the concept is understood in conventional AI work. Look back at Blocks 1 and 2 if you want.

Discussion ....

Symbolic AI is based on a certain conception of *human* intelligence, on a general understanding of the workings of our own minds. As sentient beings, we know that we bring special abilities to the world: we use language and logic to plan, communicate and carry out complex tasks; we reason about the present and the future; we respond flexibly to new situations or unexpected developments.

To sum this up, these are some of the presumed basic characteristics of human 'intelligence' in the broadest sense, characteristics that conventional AI seeks to replicate on machines:

▶ knowledge

▶ rational thought (using symbols to reason with, as in logic and mathematics)

▶ language (using symbols to communicate in speech and writing)

▶ the ability to make plans, design and foresee

▶ the ability to learn specialised knowledge and skills.

But although we might not be inclined to call ants or geese 'intelligent' in any of the above senses, something more than simple randomness is clearly taking place in the behaviour described in the case studies. So perhaps it may be necessary to try for a rather more inclusive understanding of the idea of intelligence.

Exercise 1.3

To what extent do you think a chimpanzee could be called 'intelligent'? What about a dog? An insect? Do you think there could be any alternative conceptions of 'intelligence', or is human intelligence the only sort possible?

Discussion ....

Chimpanzees might not seem to be capable of the kind of symbol manipulation that we think of as typical of the human mind. However, the evidence that they have an intelligence in many ways like our own is compelling. They live in complex social groups in which status, rank, sharing, cooperation, deception and manipulation all play a part. They make and use tools, can solve complex problems and can be taught a grasp of certain limited forms of language. It's hard to deny that they have sophisticated minds. Dogs, as we know, can learn complex tasks, display emotions, perform feats of recognition and problem solving, and learn to respond to language – of a simple kind. But we would probably balk at the idea that dogs' minds function logically or that they contain symbolically encoded knowledge. As you've seen, insects such as ants display highly organised mass behaviour, and some insects even seem to have basic learning capacities. But no one in their right mind would be inclined to call an individual insect – with its tiny, almost non-existent brain – intelligent, or to suggest it uses logic or symbols.

Clearly, the issue is a complicated one. On the one hand, few if any creatures seem to possess anything resembling the human capacity for rationality, language and knowledge. On the other hand, we see all around the natural world feats of problem solving, construction and organisation that are often startling. And the idea that humanity stands completely apart from the rest of creation, is unique and unrivalled in its status and abilities, does not sit well with the twentieth-century mind. When Shakespeare wrote in 1603:

> What a piece of work is a man! How noble in reason! how infinite in faculty! in form, in moving, how express and admirable! in action how like an angel! in apprehension how like a god! the beauty of the world! the paragon of animals!
>
> Source: Shakespeare, *Hamlet* II. ii

he was expressing the standard view of the time. This belief was expressed with blunt clarity in the words of the fifth-century church father, St Augustine:

> if, when we say, Thou shalt not kill, we do not understand this of the plants, since they have no sensation, nor of the irrational animals that fly, swim, walk, or creep, since they are dissociated from us by their want of reason, and are therefore by the just appointment of the Creator subjected to us to kill or keep alive for our own uses ...
>
> Source: St Augustine of Hippo, *The City of God*, Book I

I think few of us would be comfortable with this now. Since Darwin, we are much more inclined to see close links between ourselves and the rest of the natural world, to view our abilities and those of other creatures as all part of a continuum. And in directly comparing our minds to those of animals (usually to the animals' detriment) we may be making a deeper mistake. Many ethologists argue that such comparison leads inevitably to **anthropomorphism** – seeing intelligence only in behaviour that resembles our own, dismissing everything else as 'instinct' or some such word. But the truth is that every species is specially adapted to the specific problems that it confronts. The abilities of, say, a pigeon and a lion are simply not comparable: they inhabit quite different mental worlds. Ludwig Wittgenstein once wrote, cryptically, 'If a lion could speak, we would not understand him'. But you can see what he meant. How could we possibly understand a lion's mind? Its purposes and ours barely intersect at all.

Ethology is the comparative study of the behaviour of creatures, including humans, living in their natural environment.

Perhaps the best way to investigate this further is to consider in detail some very broad qualities that we might associate with intelligent behaviour. In my answer to Exercise 1.1, I suggested that the case studies demonstrated behaviour that is *purposeful* and *systematic* and leads to *ordered* results. In the next three subsections, I will look a little more deeply at each of these qualities and consider what they might tell us about intelligent behaviour.

3.1 Purposeful behaviour

The behaviours touched on in Case Studies 1.1 and 1.2 seem to be aimed towards some specific goal – reaching a safe environment, the recovery of prey, and so on. We can call this sort of behaviour **goal-directed**. It can be found everywhere in nature. However, we should be careful: the term can be used to cover a whole range of different cases. Consider the following three case studies.

Case Study 1.3: Tool-using primates

Most non-human anthropoid primates (monkeys, apes) construct and use tools. Chimpanzees, for instance, use sticks to break open termite nests, pick the locks of their cages, and push away dangerous or unpleasant objects that they would rather not touch; they use leaves to clean themselves and food items as bait. If one is available, they will use a stout rod to prise apart the bars of their cage so that they can put their heads out for a better view. A screwdriver dropped into a chimp's cage may be used as a spear, hammer, probe, mill, toothpick or for any other purpose the chimp can put it to. Orangutans, however, prefer to hide the screwdriver and then 'barter' it for a food reward from their keepers. Gorillas will first try to eat the screwdriver and then ignore it thereafter. However, gorillas in the wild do use sticks as weapons and, in captivity, can be taught to store water in containers.

Figure 1.5   A chimp cracks nuts with a 'hammer'

Both chimps and orangutans can make strategic use of tools to accomplish goals such as obtaining food, often devoting a lot of time and experiment to the problem. They will use sticks to reach out for food outside their cages, searching for longer sticks or even joining sticks together, if necessary, until they have an instrument long enough to rake the food towards them. If food is suspended above them they will make a stable stack of objects, or balance a pole, and then climb it to reach the goal.

Case Study 1.4: Shellfish-eating birds

The oystercatcher (*Haematopus ostralegus*) is a shorebird that feeds mainly on mussels and other shellfish foraged from the shoreline. An obvious problem for feeding behaviour of this kind is opening the shell to get at the edible parts inside. Studies of oystercatchers have revealed that they break open shells by two means:

► The shells of mussels washed up by the tide onto dry land tend to be tightly closed. In such cases, the bird will move the shell to a dry place where the sand is hard enough to provide support – soft sand will not do – turn it over so its thinner, more fragile underside is upwards, and then hammer it open with its bill.

▶ Mussel shells fished out of shallow water are generally slightly open. The oystercatchers prise the shells of these specimens open by inserting their bills into the crack and cutting the abductor muscle which holds the shell closed.

Careful observations have suggested that an individual oystercatcher specialises in one or other of the above techniques. This appears to be behaviour learned from the bird's parents.

Many species of gull open shells by dropping them on a hard surface from a height of several metres. Herring gulls (*Larus argentatus*) are particularly good at selecting suitably hard dropping zones, such as rocks, pavements and car parks, and will generally choose the right altitude from which to drop the shellfish, depending on the size of the target. If the shell fails to break, they will pick it up and try again. Crows will drop whelks only onto certain rocks, choosing their target from the point of view of size, flatness and distance from the waterline (so that edible fragments don't fall into the water); they prefer to drop from a low altitude, so that the edible parts are not widely scattered, even if this means they have to repeat the drop many times.

Case Study 1.5: Plume-tracking lobsters

The American lobster (*Homerus americanus*) inhabits rocky, shallow-water coastal habitats that provide adequate food and shelter from predators. They hunt for food at night, their diet including fish, crabs, clams, mussels, sea urchins and sometimes other lobsters. Their nocturnal behaviour, along with the fact that they only have rudimentary eyesight, means that lobsters have to rely on their highly developed sense of smell to detect prey, mates and predators. The strategy they use is known as *plume tracking*.

Lobsters use structures called antennules, as well as odour-sensitive hairs on their bodies, to detect water currents – known as plumes – bearing the smell of prey, and to aim themselves towards the source. It is now known that they use a principle called **chemotaxis**, in which they extract directional information from the composition of the plume itself to do this. How this is achieved, or precisely what information is being used, is not well understood. Somehow the lobster remains in the centre of the plume and orients itself towards the source by constantly monitoring changes in the make-up of the plume as it moves. Some researchers believe the downstroke of the anntenule, which is very fast, captures a high-resolution picture of the plume's structure, while the slower upstroke measures and analyses that structure.

On the face of it, these all seem to be examples of goal-directed behaviour. But let's consider how they compare.

Exercise 1.4

Given all these cases involve trying to achieve a goal, what differences do you think there are between them? Try to think about the goals themselves as well as the behaviour that leads towards them. What part do you think *reasoning* might play in these activities?

Discussion ....

I think that there is a clear *hierarchy* of complexity here, moving from very simple to extremely intricate behaviour. To take the cases in reverse order:

1   In Case Study 1.5, the lobster is sensing its environment, doing some internal processing, recognising a stimulus of interest, and then adjusting its responses accordingly, to support its primary purposes of feeding, hiding or mating.

2   The behaviour of the gulls in Case Study 1.4 is more clearly recognisable as goal-directed and appears more sophisticated. The primary goal is still simple – to feed;

but in this case the birds' behaviour is underpinned by refined sensory recognition systems (estimating the position and geometry of the shell, identifying the right type of rock, judging the texture of the sand) and flexible behaviour (choosing the right height for the drop, dropping the shell again, if necessary).

3   Chimpanzees are our nearest relatives genetically, so in Case Study 1.3 we find behaviour that we could have no qualms about labelling as 'intelligent'. The apes may have a simple goal – a banana – but in other cases it can be more complex and abstract, such as wanting to have a more interesting view, freedom from the cage, and so on. Even more impressively, the chimp can work out how to reach its goal through a series of *stages*, or *subgoals*.

Although these three cases are, of course, very different, it's difficult to see where one could draw a clear line between goal-directed behaviour that is 'intelligent' and that which isn't. The chimps' mentality seems to resemble our own. They have abstract goals, they form plans, they appear to have an excellent grasp of causality: for example, they know, after a bit of thought and experiment, that certain actions will lead to given results (*if* I use the rod in this way, *then* the bars will bend). However, be aware of a temptation towards anthropomorphism here. It's tempting to label gorillas as less 'intelligent' than chimpanzees, as they show little interest in, or desire to use, tools. But gorillas are herbivores, living in the wild on a simple and abundant diet of nettles and leaves. They would have little use for tools and, presumably, have not evolved to recognise or use them.

But what about the gulls and the lobsters? It would seem quite reasonable to call the lobster's plume tracking goal-directed, even though it is still a fairly straightforward form of stimulus and response that biologists call **taxis**. Of course, it's hard to imagine that lobsters (which are related to spiders) have any awareness of pursuing an aim, but their behaviour is quite intricately purposeful, nevertheless. The gulls and crows are even more problematic. At one time, it was common to dismiss this type of behaviour as 'instinctive' (as if that explained it away), but repeated experiments have shown that it is learned. What we can clearly see in these cases is the pursuit of basic goals (feeding, etc.) through complex, flexible behaviour.

It's important to reiterate the main point here: none of these creatures possesses a developed language, as humans do, and none of them, with the possible exception of the chimps, could be said to be *reasoning* about their goals. Chimpanzees can be taught restricted versions of human language, but it's doubtful whether they perform anything like the sort of symbolic reasoning that you encountered in Block 2. So goal-directed behaviour can occur, and be effective, even in the absence of logic and symbols. And it surely seems reasonable to see goal-directed behaviour as lying along a *spectrum* of complexity and sophistication, from the purely mechanical reactions we see in plants through to the complexity of human goals and plans.

3.2   Systematic behaviour

One of the most striking features of army ant attacks, described in Case Study 1.2, is just how *organised* they are. Raids begin at the same time of day; the swarm front develops in an apparently disciplined fashion; individual ants specialise in specific tasks; prey items are butchered and returned methodically to the bivouac – the whole collective seems to act with the obedience and control of an army. We noted similarly orderly behaviour in the migration of birds. In all cases the animals seem to be behaving *systematically*, with a regularity that is quite unlike the piling up of rocks by a glacier or the flow of a river.

Here is another example of such systematic activity in nature.

Case Study 1.6: Nest-building paper wasps

The paper wasp (*Polybia occidentalis*) is a social insect that lives in large colonies and builds elaborate nests (see Figure 1.6). When a swarm, made up of one or more queens and many thousands of workers, arrives at a nesting site, nest construction starts with a set of hexagonal brood cells attached to a suitable support, such as a twig. The workers gradually extend this comb of cells outwards to form a disc shape, projecting either side of the support. The queen begins laying eggs in these cells more or less as soon as the construction of the comb starts, and a number of workers immediately take on the task of removing corpses and faeces from them.

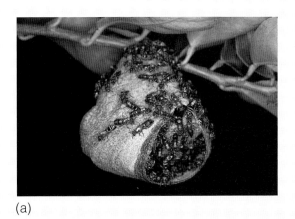

(a)

(b)

Figure 1.6   (a) Envelope construction is nearly complete. You can see some of the comb cells inside. (b) Workers begin a new comb on the underside of the previous envelope

When the comb has reached a certain size, the behaviour of the building workers changes abruptly; they move back to near the point of attachment of the comb and start constructing a dome-shaped protective envelope around it (see Figure 1.6(a)). The envelope is extended to completely enclose the comb, apart from an access hole about 1 centimetre wide. As the envelope is finally closed off, building behaviour changes again and the workers start to assemble a new comb of brood cells, attached to the underside of the envelope they have just completed (see Figure 1.6(b)). Once again, when this new comb reaches a certain size, a new enclosing envelope is started. The workers continue to alternate between building combs and envelopes until the nest is big enough for the whole swarm and their brood. The nest may be extended later, and is kept in good repair for as long as the colony occupies it.

Both combs and envelopes are constructed from pulped wood that is moistened and then allowed to dry. Two groups of specialised workers forage for the necessary materials, one for wood pulp and one for water, while a third group does the building. It appears that no wasp is irrevocably committed to one task only: a worker in one group may switch to one of the others, but this does not happen frequently. The activities of the three groups are very closely coordinated. Water foragers supply water to both builders and pulp foragers, who use it to moisten wood pulp. Wood-pulp foragers supply material just to builders. The size of the three groups changes constantly, according to the building needs of the moment; and, in some way, these relative sizes change to minimise queuing delays.

3.3 Structured and functional results

While the paper wasps provide another example of goal-directed, systematic behaviour, perhaps this case study's most noteworthy feature is that not only is the activity of the wasps decidedly regular and methodical, but the end result is also highly *structured*. There are countless other examples we could cite of animals building serviceable, complex structures – shelters, nests and colonies, specialised tools, and devices to catch prey. Such constructions are all highly *functional*: they appear beautifully fashioned to serve the particular purpose they were built for. The end product perfectly serves the original goal.

Structure and function are qualities we associate with human artefacts. Nature tends to deal in chaotic, fractal patterns. Most of you will have flown high over the land in a jet airliner and observed the scene below: rivers, mountains and lakes are jagged and irregular in shape. The regular outlines of fields, roads and canals tell us that human activity has shaped the landscape. And all around us are countless examples of human purpose: buildings, dams, machines, the software we are using to write this course. These constructions are triumphs of humanity's ingenuity and planning. An example I can't resist giving is the breathtaking new Milau suspension bridge in southern France, opened in 2005. With seven piers spanning a total of 2.5 kilometres across the gorge of the River Tarn, it towers 336 metres above the valley floor, making it the highest bridge in the world (higher than the Eiffel Tower). It took over three years to build and cost €394 million.

Figure 1.7   The Milau suspension bridge

Complex entities such as these come about through the process that we call *engineering*. Now, although you probably feel fairly certain you know what engineering is, it's worth giving a moment's thought to the concept.

Exercise 1.5

Imagine you were the manager of the project to build the Milau bridge. Write brief notes on how you might start tackling this problem. I'm assuming you are not an engineer, so I wouldn't expect a very detailed answer here. Try to give an outline of the approach you would take.

Discussion ....

Clearly a system this size couldn't possibly be built by one person alone, so you would need to appoint a team. This in turn implies that the work will have to be divided up into parts (design, materials, logistics and planning, testing and quality assurance, for example). Possibly one team member could be placed in charge of each part, and each of them would certainly also want to divide their particular task into work units. You would then have to allocate time and resources to each task and fix deadlines for them. You would probably want to draw up a project timeline and use techniques like critical path analysis to predict areas of possible future difficulty. All subtasks of the main units would also have to be costed and allocated time and deadlines. You would need to set up a strong system of reporting and monitoring to follow the day-to-day running of the project.

This is what we might call an engineering approach. Engineering is, of course, concerned with building complex things, usually physical things such as dams and bridges (although software engineers, by contrast, build an intangible entity – software). What I think distinguishes it from other activities that involve making things – cookery, flower arranging, and so on – is that it has to be a highly *disciplined* and *systematic* activity. Engineers must plan meticulously, produce careful designs, choose the most suitable materials, conform with all the relevant standards and practices, and work within firm margins of time and money. They will use scientific, technical and mathematical techniques to support this work. One could hardly imagine a more clear-cut example of human intelligence at work. The whole process is obviously ordered and systematic, as one would expect.

However, perhaps the most noticeable feature of this strategy is its **top-down organisation**. A single directing intelligence sits at the top of a hierarchy of tasks and control. Work is divided into units, which are in turn divided into subunits and become the responsibility of other guiding minds. *Information* flows up the hierarchy and *control*, in the shape of decisions and instructions, passes down it. This pattern will be immediately recognisable to you as computer programmers. Many software systems, particularly those built in the earlier days of computing, are structured in exactly this top-down pattern. The design of the systems we build often mirrors the structure of the processes we use to build them.

Exercise 1.6

There are obvious differences between the activity of an engineer and that of nest-building wasps. Quickly note down what you think these differences are. Do you think there are any similarities?

Discussion ....

The only similarities I could see between the two cases are that both activities are purposeful, systematic and lead to structured, functional results. As I suggested above, engineering is a disciplined activity that involves planning and design, and is underpinned by the symbolic language of mathematics. Even where mathematical calculation is not involved, the engineer will rely on design drawings and written documentation, both also forms of symbolic representation. It seems incredibly unlikely that the wasps plan their work. Obviously they have no designs to work from, in any sense that we could understand the term. And mathematics must surely be far beyond the reach of an insect.

So there can be no doubt at all that wasps are not engineers. Yet they behave systematically to produce a regular structure, perfectly fitted to the task it is built for. Of course, it would be idle to pretend that the wasps are making anything as complex as the Milau bridge. However, there are similarities between the two cases. Both the human and the insect activity give rise to a structured and functional end-product. And both cases involve a number of independent workers whose activities have to be closely coordinated.

Nevertheless, despite the similarities, there is a sharp contrast between the two cases. Engineering is a top-down, human approach to a complex problem; the wasps seem to be following a radically different path. There is no overall control, no managing brain, no design, no obvious breakdown of tasks. We refer to this sort of organisation as **bottom-up**. The coordination of the wasps' work can't possibly come about in the same way as that of the human engineers – the necessary mechanisms simply aren't available. For a start there is no overall controller: the medieval notion that the queen's role is somehow like that of a human sovereign is a fantasy; queens simply lay eggs. And even if there was some important wasp in charge, there are no obvious ways it could communicate orders to the rest of the swarm. Insects do communicate, as we shall see later, but nevertheless there is no practical means by which messages could reach the widely distributed builders and foragers. However, the insects do seem to work together remarkably effectively, with convincingly practical results.

Our tendency to take regular, functional structures to be evidence of superior intelligence at work was perfectly expressed by William Paley (1734–1805), in the following very well-known observation from his *Natural Theology* of 1800. He asks us to imagine walking on a heath and striking one's foot against an object we think at first is a stone, but which on closer examination turns out to be a watch. He goes on:

> ... when we come to inspect the watch, we perceive ... that its several parts are framed and put together for a purpose, e.g. that they are so formed and adjusted as to produce motion, and that motion so regulated as to point out the hour of the day; that if the different parts had been differently shaped from what they are, or placed after any other manner or in any other order than that in which they are placed, either no motion at all would have been carried on in the machine, or none which would have answered the use that is now served by it ... the inference we think is inevitable, that the watch must have had a maker – that there must have existed, at some time and at some place or other, an artificer or artificers who formed it for the purpose which we find it actually to answer, who comprehended its construction and designed its use.
>
> Source: Paley (1800), Chapter 1

Figure 1.8   William Paley

How simple creatures such as wasps, without engineering devices such as planning, design or mathematical reasoning, and presumably without having 'comprehended its structure and designed its use', can produce something as ordered and functional as a nest is a question I will start to try to tackle in the next unit. Let's now try to round off this discussion of natural intelligence, first with a brief recap and then with some conclusions.

SAQ 1.2

Write brief definitions of *goal-directed* behaviour, *systematic* behaviour and *structured* and *functional results*, as they've appeared in this section, giving one example of each.

ANSWER..

Goal directedness is simply acting in such a way as to reach some clearly defined objective, such as when a homing pigeon flies back to a fixed place, or an animal forages for food. I've given a number of examples of behaviour that is systematic – that is, it seems to follow a pattern or some fairly rigid process: organised hunting behaviour, systematic construction of nests and shelters, etc. Lastly, I noted that such systematic activity can result in highly regular and functional products, structures perfectly suited for a particular purpose.

3.4 | Some conclusions

See Griffin (2001), from which many of my examples have been taken.

Some naturalists and ethologists insist that animals are completely without thought, mentality or conscious awareness. A few others, such as Donald Griffin, believe that even quite simple creatures may have mental states comparable in kind to our own. The majority do not want to commit themselves, but generally avoid questions about animals' mental life with distaste, on the grounds that mental states cannot be observed directly, so talk of them is unscientific. Boakes writes:

> ... attributing conscious thought to animals should be strenuously avoided in any serious attempt to understand their behaviour, since it is untestable, empty, obstructionist and based on a false dichotomy ...
>
> Source: Boakes (1992) 'Subjective Experience', *Times Higher Education Supplement*

Fortunately, we do not need to take sides in this debate, which I think has been bedevilled by misunderstanding, prejudice and muddled thinking. Animals may, or may not, be consciously aware of what they are doing. The main point I've been trying to make in my choice of case studies is simpler. It is that *behaviour* we would be inclined to label 'intelligent' can be seen on a continuum: Einstein was intelligent; we would almost certainly want to say that the chimpanzee using a tool to get at a banana is acting intelligently. Clearly a plant isn't intelligent – how could it have a mind in any conceivable sense? But what about migrating birds? nest-building wasps? foraging gulls? It seems irrational to draw a firm line somewhere in nature and say 'here intelligence begins'. And it is surely anthropomorphic to draw that line under *Homo sapiens* and exclude all else.

Every organism in the natural world has problems to solve – what David Attenborough once called 'the trials of life': how to find food; how to avoid *becoming* food; how to find a mate; how to navigate safely around a hostile and dangerous world. All existing animals have devised workable, if imperfect, solutions to these problems. And so computer scientist Luc Steels has defined intelligence as 'success in self-preservation'. Now it seems most unlikely that wasps reason about how to build their nests or consult blueprints; birds do not have printed maps to guide them; nor do ants have charts of their territory or control their armies with orders. No animals other than humans appear to have language in any truly developed sense. Still less (I believe) does nature itself have a rational plan for its own development. But nature has found ingenious answers to the trials of life. It has its own forms of intelligence.

All of our case studies were chosen to suggest that this **natural intelligence** – if we understand the term in a suitably liberal sense – may be widespread in nature, and that anthropomorphic definitions of the idea might not tell the whole story. My aim now is to move away from, and to contrast, the general idea of 'intelligence' implicit in Block 2's approach to artificial intelligence, as being exclusively *human* intelligence.

SAQ 1.3

Try to recall some of the characteristics of human intelligence that AI seeks to represent and replicate on machines.

ANSWER...

Earlier in this unit we came up with the following list:

▶ knowledge

▶ rational thought (using symbols to reason with, as in logic and mathematics)

▶ language (using symbols to communicate in speech and writing)

▶ the ability to make plans, design and foresee

▶ the ability to learn specialised knowledge and skills.

Looking back at Block 2, you might have been able to come up with some other plausible ideas.

Now, let's try to use this to draw some conclusions about natural intelligence from what we have learned so far. If we can agree that, in general terms, intelligence can be recognised in activities that appear goal-directed, systematic and ordered, what might this suggest about animal intelligence?

Exercise 1.7

Look back at Case Studies 1.1 to 1.6. What mental or behavioural capacities do you think the various animals discussed there would need to produce the goal-directed, systematic behaviour we observed? Based on your general knowledge, can you think of any additional abilities that might be necessary, and that some animals may possess? Try to think clearly about the case studies and develop a broad conception of intelligence, one that doesn't presuppose logic, language or formal, explicit thought.

Discussion ....

This is probably the most challenging exercise I've asked of you so far. However, I think it is definitely worth carrying out. I arrived at six mental and behavioural characteristics that I thought were demonstrated, at some level or other, by most of the animals in the nine case studies: drives, recognition, classification, response, communication and learning.

You may have come out with different ideas, but let's look at each of these six in a little more detail and extend our analysis beyond the human sphere.

Drives. At the root of every form of animal behaviour there seem to be basic drives. Living creatures have purposes in what they do. We are all familiar with the complexity of human motives. Why am I writing this course? Naturally, I want to earn money to eke out my paltry existence; but I also have other, less tangible reasons – creativity, professional pride, desire to convey ideas I think are interesting, and so on. Why are you studying M366? Presumably, your purposes are many and various. Animal drives tend to be simpler, of course. At the root of everything lies the battle for *survival*, which can be boiled down to what the philosopher Dan Dennett once memorably called the four Fs: feeding, fleeing, fighting and finding a mate. Without drives, intelligent behaviour – or behaviour of any sort other than randomness – simply wouldn't happen.

Recognition. In the case studies, we noted that birds navigate with reference to stars and landmarks, lobsters detect prey in waterborne plumes, etc. Even the humblest creatures sense their environment: single-celled amoebae are sensitive to light, for instance. But with increasing sophistication comes an increasing ability to recognise and discriminate. A lobster can tell the difference between a plume given off by a predator and one indicating a possible mate. Herring gulls can tell the right type of dropping zone from the air. Chimps recognise each other as individuals. In all these cases, what the animal is identifying is a complex *pattern* of features – a special configuration of stars, or a suitable combination of flatness, hardness and physical position relative to the waterline in a rock. This ability to recognise patterns as a whole will be a topic of major importance in the course.

Classification. Along with this ability to recognise, comes the related ability to *classify* or *categorise* the things that are sensed. We've seen in the case studies that migrating birds can distinguish some landmarks and constellations from others; lobsters can classify plumes into friend or foe. In a very well-known experiment, a plane towed the basic shape illustrated in Figure 1.9 across the sky above fields in which birds were feeding. If the object was towed in orientation (a), the feeding birds below took no notice – the moving shape resembled a harmless goose. However, when towed in orientation (b) the shape immediately came to resemble a predatory hawk, and the birds below all went into avoidance and hiding behaviour. Clearly they were able to classify shapes at least into the simple categories 'dangerous' and 'harmless'.

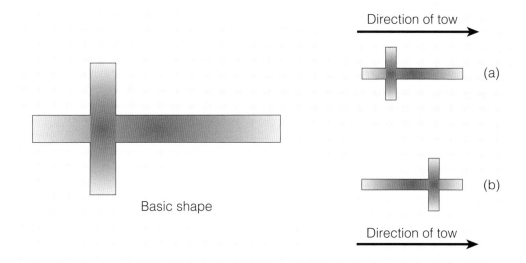

Figure 1.9   Bird recognition and classification experiment

Humans deal with the complexities of the world by means of an intricate system of *concepts*, in which whole families of phenomena are classified under one label – for example, the tag 'tree' covers the entire vast collection of things we call trees. This ability to categorise seems to be related to our capacity for language. We use a semantic marker, a word, to stand for a whole mass of features and individuals. Whether animals can have a conceptual system of any sort is a matter of fierce debate among ethologists and behavioural psychologists. No animals have a language of any sophistication, so if they have any system of concepts at all it is bound to be limited. Various experimenters have reported work in which chimps can be taught to count numerical sequences. Pigeons can learn to discriminate between categories such as 'picture with a person in it' and 'picture without a person in it', and even between some geometric shapes presented in various sizes and orientations. But there is little agreement over how such results should be interpreted, and the whole question is clouded by anthropomorphism, as the case of 'Clever Hans', which I'll discuss below in Case Study 1.7, indicates.

Response. By this I mean rather more than the fact that animals react appropriately to the stimuli they receive. A simple creature like a lobster or an ant seems to have a fairly limited range of responses it can make: the lobster, for example, when it detects a plume, can choose to move towards it or away from it. However, although such reactions may appear straightforward at first sight, they conceal deep complexity. As I stated, it is by no means understood how the lobster maintains itself in the centre of the plume and selects the right direction to move in. And consider the elementary action of catching a ball: we wouldn't be inclined to call it intelligent – anyone can do it. Dogs can be trained to do it. But, although we aren't aware of it, we are performing complex calculations in real time as we move to make that clean catch. Even actions to which we would not give a single thought, such as walking and handling objects, turn out to be massively complicated processes, as you will see in the next unit.

But the most important point here is that animals are *active*. They move around the world; they are intimately involved with it; they are constantly required to respond to its demands; and they shape it to suit their needs. It is in this activity that the roots of intelligence lie. In his science fiction novel of 1930, *Last and First Men*, Olaf Stapledon pictured a future time in which humanity decides to construct several huge brains, without bodies, suspended in vats, intended to solve all the problems of knowledge through pure intellect:

> Man, they said, is a very noble organism. We have dealt with other organisms so as to enhance in each its noblest attributes. It is time to do the same with man. What is most distinctive in man is intelligent manipulation, brain and hand. Now hand is really outclassed by modern mechanisms, but brain will never be outclassed. Therefore we must breed strictly for brain ... We must produce an organism that will be no mere bundle of relics left over from its primitive ancestors precariously ruled by a glimmer of intelligence. We must produce a man who is nothing but man ...
>
> The governing caste were strongly opposed to this policy ... Man, they said, was essentially an animal, though uniquely gifted. His whole nature must be developed, not just one faculty at the expense of others ...
>
> Source: Stapledon (1930) *Last and First Men*, p. 208

So it proves. The great disembodied brains are built, but:

> [the great brains] had a growing sense that though in a manner they knew almost everything, they really knew nothing.
>
> The normal mind, when it experiences intellectual frustration, can seek recreation in companionship, or physical exercise, or art. But for [the brains] there was no such escape. These activities were impossible or meaningless to them ...
>
> Ibid., p. 215

But actually it would be much worse than this. A brain without a body could never have evolved intelligence. It would not think at all, for it would have nothing to think about.

Communication. I didn't stress this in my discussions of the case studies but it is certainly implied in them. Some of those animals work together *collectively* – the ants and, to some extent, the birds. We will look more deeply at such communal behaviour early in the next unit, but it seems fairly obvious that cooperative action couldn't be achieved without some form of communication between individuals. Many animals do have elementary 'languages' – systems of signalling to one another. But without syntax, subtle semantics or verbal association, these have nothing remotely resembling the power of our languages.

Learning. Again, this did not appear explicitly in the case studies. However, remember that migrating birds have been shown to learn the shapes of the constellations and landmarks by which they navigate; and oystercatchers discover their feeding preferences from their parents. Learning seems crucial for intelligence. An animal that is inflexible, that has no capacity to change in response to experience, will be a poor contender in the struggle for existence. We'll return to this point in the next unit. Learning will be a major issue in the remainder of the course.

Now let's use an SAQ to consolidate these ideas.

SAQ 1.4

Look back at the six case studies and for each of them note down which, among the above six characteristics, seem to be necessary for the behaviour portrayed.

ANSWER...

My answer is as follows:

1   Case Study 1.1: drives, recognition, response and communication – probably classification and learning;

2   Case Study 1.2: drives, recognition, response and communication – classification and learning are possible but unlikely;

3   Case Study 1.3: drives, recognition, classification, response and learning – communication is not implied by the particular case study, but we know that chimps, which are gregarious animals, have sophisticated forms of communication and can even be taught the rudiments of human language;

4   Case Study 1.4: drives, recognition, classification, response and learning;

5   Case Study 1.5: drives, recognition, classification and response;

6   Case Study 1.6: drives, recognition, classification, response and communication.

You may have come up with rather different ideas; the whole area is difficult because we are having to *infer* mental properties (if animals have mental properties at all) from outward behaviour.

3.5   A dreadful warning

Finally, a case study to serve as a warning against the ever-present danger of anthropomorphism.

Case Study 1.7: 'Clever Hans'

Hans von Osten lived in Berlin around the turn of the nineteenth century and was famous throughout Germany for his ability to solve mathematical problems such as 3×4 or 3×9. Not so special, you might think – but 'Clever Hans' was a horse. His owner, Herr von Osten, would write an expression such as 2×3 or 5×2 on a blackboard and Hans would respond by tapping the ground with his hoof the right number of times. He sometimes got the answer wrong, but his success rate was much higher than chance. People came from far and wide to watch Hans's act and many scientists of the time accepted that he understood arithmetic and could calculate.

Exercise 1.8

What do you think? Are other explanations possible? Did Hans understand arithmetic? Could he calculate?

Discussion ....

Alas, no. The psychologist Oskar Pfungst was able to show that Hans was not even looking at the blackboard, which we may assume meant nothing to him. He was watching his master. He had learned to pick up tiny, unnoticed scraps of body language which told him when was the moment to stop tapping his hoof. If no one was present as the problem was presented, he simply tapped at random.

Earlier in this unit we defined *anthropomorphism* as a tendency to call behaviour 'intelligent' only if we can identify it with our own. Anthropomorphism is an ever-present danger when we try to make inferences about animal intelligence. Here we have an inverted case of the same problem. Looking at Hans's behaviour, it is all too easy to imagine he had mental states – an awareness of number and sequence, an appreciation of the meaning of arithmetic operators – which he simply did not possess. He was a horse. The mental world of horses, if they have one at all, must surely be utterly remote from ours.

3.6 Natural, artificial, living

Natural and artificial things

So far, we have been looking at intelligence in the natural world. At this point in the discussion, it is worth pausing briefly to consider whether intelligence is exclusive to nature and natural systems. If it isn't, where else might intelligence be found? This seems a reasonable question, given that our goal is to build intelligent computer-based systems – artificial systems with intelligent capacities. But what exactly *is* an 'artificial system'? What does it mean for something to be 'artificial', as opposed to 'natural'?

'Nature' can be defined in countless different ways. The character of each definition is largely determined by who is proposing it (for example, a philosopher or a biologist) and the purposes for which it is intended. This section will give you an idea of the wide-ranging and often conflicting ways in which philosophers and scientists have interpreted the idea of 'nature'.

Exercise 1.9

Spend the next few minutes trying to come up with your own definition of the term 'nature'.

Discussion ....

You might have come up with one or more of the definitions in the following list (which is not intended to be exhaustive):

▶ the essence of a thing, its core or 'inner' reality: as in, for instance, the statement 'by his very nature, he is cautious';

▶ the sum of all natural things – you can probably see at once that this definition is circular: nature is defined in terms of the natural, which remains undefined;

▶ all the things in the world that have originated without human influence;

▶ all living things, either including or excluding humans;

▶ the structures, processes and laws that make up the world, which are studied in the natural sciences and which scientists, technologists and engineers seek to harness or to modify.

For our purposes, we might perhaps settle on this smaller set of definitions proposed by Frederick Ferré in *The Philosophy of Technology* (1988):

1   nature as all that exists in the evolving world of space and time;

2   nature as that which is essential in a thing, that is, that which is expressed, all other things being equal, when it develops according to its kind without outside interference;

3   nature as the collective term for all that exists apart from the artificial.

SAQ 1.5

Read over Ferré's three definitions again. Do you detect any problem with them when they are taken together?

ANSWER..

You may have spotted that the set of definitions is inconsistent: definition 1 states that nature is everything that exists, which would have to include all artificial things, yet the artificial is explicitly excluded from nature in definition 3.

Clearly, either everything is part of nature, in which case the artificial cannot be something 'other' than nature, or everything is not part of nature, in which case there is a distinction between nature and the artificial. If we want to make this distinction, then we have an obvious duty to define what we mean by 'artificial'.

In his book *The Sciences of the Artificial* (1981), the pioneering computer scientist Herb Simon, whom you met in Block 2, identifies the following list of features as characteristic of artificial systems:

▶   They are constructed (though not always, or even usually, with full forethought) by man.

▶   They may imitate the appearances of natural things but lack, in one or many respects, their reality.

▶   They can be characterised in terms of functions, goals and adaptation.

▶   They are often discussed, particularly when being designed, in terms of imperatives (that is, in terms of how a thing *ought* to be) as well as descriptives (that is, in terms of how a thing actually *is*).

Simon maintains that the artificial arises from applying human rationality to the design of objects. If this rational design process is somehow analogous to evolution, then artificial things in some ways resemble natural things. There are clear echoes here of Paley's argument, which you met earlier in Section 3.2 of this unit. Most higher organisms give the impression of having been superbly designed for their various purposes. However, the majority of scientists don't accept the theory of intelligent design. They see structure, order and pattern as arising from blind, impersonal forces – through evolution or other processes. So although we are usually inclined to see the products of human activity as 'artificial' and animals and plants as 'natural', for Simon the distinction breaks down. In his view, artefacts are designed by humans: organisms are designed by nature.

The boundary between artificial and natural becomes even more blurred when we turn from the rational, top-down design of artificial things, such as bridges or computer programs, to the bottom-up design of artificial things by means of techniques that are inspired by natural processes, such as Darwinian evolution by natural selection. I will return to this issue in Unit 2 of this block. Constructing complex artificial objects using processes based on Darwinian evolution is the main theme of Block 5.

Living things

Throughout this unit, we've been discussing animals and plants as living things, members of a distinct, biological kingdom, as if it was self-evident what life actually *is*, and that the distinction between living things (such as parrots, spiders and humans) and artefacts (such as bridges, spoons and computers) is clear cut. At first glance, the distinction does seem self-evident: surely we all believe that there is a sharp division between systems that are biological, or living, on the one hand, and non-biological, or inanimate, on the other. We would generally have no trouble in assigning an anteater to the first and a computer to the second.

But, as so often, such a clear and obvious separation may not stand rather closer scrutiny. Think about this difficult question.

Exercise 1.10

What makes something 'biological'? What makes it 'living' as distinguished from something that is 'non-biological' and 'non-living'? This is a huge question, so don't dwell on it for too long. Just jot down one or two possible answers.

Discussion ....

Arriving at a hard and fast definition of 'life' as a basis for distinguishing living from non-living things has proved very difficult, if not impossible. The *Oxford English Dictionary* defines 'biology' as 'the science of physical life', but this hardly helps: it's another piece of circularity. Some scientists would want to say that biological systems depend on complex interactions between certain types of organic molecules, notably DNA, amino acids and proteins. They might offer a rough definition of a living thing as one that shows evidence of all of the following at least once during its existence:

► growth

► metabolism: it maintains itself by taking in, storing and using energy and expelling waste

► motion

► response to stimuli

► reproduction.

Unfortunately, as you can probably see, these definitions can easily be broken down by counterexamples. A cast-iron definition of 'life', and even of 'biology', has eluded science. Certainly, all known biology depends on certain complex organic molecules, but so do many other systems that we would not consider to be alive. Crystals grow; my laptop computer takes in energy, stores it, uses it for computations and radiates waste in the form of heat. Cars move under their own steam; and thermostats respond to changes in their environment. Viruses, which are only questionably alive, reproduce themselves.

According to *The Oxford Companion to Philosophy*:

> Efforts to find some distinctive substance characterizing life have proven as futile as they have been heroic. The one thing which is clear is that any analysis of life must accept and appreciate that there will be many borderline instances, like viruses.

Source: *The Oxford Companion to Philosophy* (1995)

Many scientists believe that the definition-of-life question is a red herring. Life, they say, exists on a *continuum*. There are no simple alive/not-alive decisions to be made. A rock would certainly be low on any continuum of aliveness; a dog, a tree and a human would rank highly. Some systems would fall in a middle region of semi-aliveness – below bacteria, which almost everyone agrees are alive, and some way above rocks. Viruses would fall somewhere in the upper reaches of this middle ground. Below them would be complex systems that no one really considers to be alive but that display some behaviours consistent with living organisms – things such as the economy and cars.

The observation that all living things are built on an organic substrate is not particularly useful either. There are no grounds for asserting that biology *must* depend on organic molecules: some scientists call this belief **carbon chauvinism**. Indeed, one could make a persuasive case for the idea that the more sophisticated kinds of computer viruses also fit most definitions of life: they certainly move, respond, reproduce and share the metabolic properties of the computer, although there is nothing organic about them. But ordinary common sense would seem to insist that they cannot be alive.

These discussions are not irrelevant to the concept of artificial intelligence. If we accept that the distinction between 'natural' and 'artificial', 'biological' and 'non-biological' is not clear-cut, that natural things don't necessarily have to be built on an organic substrate, and that intelligence, in the sense of successful, goal-directed, problem-solving behaviour, is widespread in the natural world, then a study of how intelligence (of this broader kind) comes about could have profound implications for the kinds of systems that computer scientists write.

We can now move on to explore some of these implications.

Natural and artificial intelligence

In this unit so far, you've read three sections and seven case studies, puzzled over ten exercises and answered five SAQs – and all with scarcely a mention of *computers*. Plenty on natural intelligence, almost nothing about *artificial* intelligence. But we are computer scientists, and now is the time to set that right. Our aim is to build intelligent machines. In this final section I want to extend the discussion of computer intelligence in the light of what you've learned so far about natural intelligence. This will lead us to consider the possibility of novel techniques; yield fresh insights into old problems; and suggest how new problems might be brought within the scope of artificial intelligence. My analysis should set the stage for the rest of the course.

4.1 Intelligence and knowledge

Most computer systems are written in response to some kind of requirement, for instance the need to process text efficiently or to move robots around, or as a means to answer complex questions. Just to take a few examples at random, the following questions are all ones which we might design computer systems to answer:

▶ What are the names of all the employees who are left-handed and speak Mandarin Chinese?

▶ What would be the effect on profits of increasing production by 5%?

▶ What will the weather be like tomorrow?

Now, as you know, computers solve any problem by stepping through a suitable algorithm. For many requirements, such as sorting, searching or mathematical operations, there are well-known algorithms that work efficiently in real time. Some problems succumb to the 'brute force' algorithms I mentioned in Block 1. However, as Block 2 illustrated, many serious problems seem to require processes into which some measure of 'intelligence' has been blended, if they are to be solved within realistic timescales – or at all.

SAQ 1.6

Give two specific examples of problems that conventional artificial intelligence programs have been written to solve.

ANSWER..

All sorts of answers are possible, and many of them were discussed in Block 2. Computer translation, expert diagnosis, planning, robotic movement, etc. all come to mind here.

As discussed in Section 3, Block 2 presented the AI approach to automating processes requiring intelligence. I've argued that this originates from an anthropocentric picture of intelligence, one based on knowledge and reasoning.

SAQ 1.7

Sum up the two main principles, discussed in Block 2, that guide the construction of conventional artificial intelligence programs.

ANSWER..

Representation (explicit representation of knowledge in some symbolic form) and **search**.

The AI story is that we are able to understand the workings of our cognition by looking into our own minds, representing what we find there in some formal way, and then translating this representation into a symbolic form that can be handled by a computer. However, a moment's introspection should convince us that there are limits to introspection itself.

Consider this case. One technique still widely used in AI is to represent human knowledge as a series of production rules of the form:

```
IF ...
THEN ...
```

You looked at some examples of this in Block 2. Human experts – doctors, chemists, geologists – are quizzed in lengthy sessions of **knowledge elicitation** to draw out their knowledge and represent it in the rule-like **formalism** shown above. This can then be transferred to a computer where it can be processed by algorithms.

However, now consider another human activity, one in which most of us are 'expert': riding a bicycle. What are the rules for doing that? Clearly, we could sit together all day and you wouldn't be able to tell me. It just doesn't seem to be the sort of thing that can be expressed as rules – or expressed at all, really. We just do it. It doesn't appear to involve any explicit thought at all.

Exercise 1.11

Try to think of two similar activities you carry out without apparent thought.

Discussion ....

Examples are: walking, catching a ball, swimming, etc.

In fact, everyday human living comprises countless activities that we seem to carry out without any reasoning at all. Of course, we had to learn to do them at some time. But this learning process didn't really resemble formal teaching, of the kind you're undergoing now. I certainly didn't learn to walk by being taught the rules of ambulation.

AI stresses the importance of *knowledge*. But as you learned in Unit 1 of Block 2, knowledge is not necessarily a single kind of thing. Philosophers have long distinguished between two kinds of knowledge: propositional and non-propositional. These two can be understood as follows:

▶ **Propositional knowledge** is knowledge that can be expressed explicitly in the form of propositions, such as 'The Battle of Hastings was in 1066', or 'The light from distant galaxies shows a red shift.' It is sometimes called '*knowing that*', since you can precede each proposition with the phrase 'I know that ... (the sun rises in the east)'.

▶ **Non-propositional knowledge** is knowledge that can't be expressed in this way, usually because it is manifested in some form of ability or skill. Examples include 'I know how to swim', 'I know how to speak French', etc. So non-propositional knowledge is often called 'knowing how'.

Non-propositional knowledge is also sometimes called **tacit** or **implicit**. Other classifications have been attempted, but I won't consider them here.

SAQ 1.8

Give two examples of propositional knowledge you possess, and two of non-propositional.

ANSWER..

I know that Java is an object-oriented programming language and that Shakespeare wrote *King Lear*. I know how to swim and how to speak English.

The last example is worthy of a moment's discussion, since language is so close to the heart of our intelligence. More or less every normally reared human acquires language. Human languages are fiendishly complicated, *rule-governed* structures – without rules of some kind, a language could hardly be a language. However, if I were to ask an average speaker to *state* the rules of their language, it's very unlikely they would be able to do so. Only professional grammarians really have any explicit knowledge of linguistic rules, and even then they seldom agree. So speaking a language seems to be a matter of following rules without even knowing (propositionally) what those rules are! It is a classic example of non-propositional knowledge – at the core of our mental life.

4.2 Nouvelle AI

We needn't argue over what proportion of human knowledge is non-propositional. It's enough to say that an immense mass of human knowledge and faculties, much of it central to our lives, seems to be tacit in this way. It cannot be reached by introspection. Most of the workings of the human mind are hidden from us. The majority of psychologists would agree that what you see when you look into your own mind is only a small fraction of it. The explicit, rational, symbolic part of our minds is only the thin, visible surface layer of an ocean of cognition.

The argument in this unit has been this: look at nature and everywhere you will find cases of *non-propositional* forms of intelligence. Animals solve problems constantly, without any need for symbolic reasoning. We do too, although we are symbolic reasoners as well. An understanding of this natural intelligence might help us, as computer scientists, with some of the problems that conventional AI has failed to solve. If we can work out how goal-directed, systematic, ordered problem-solving behaviour arises in the absence of rationality and planning; if we can make sense of the mechanisms that allow both animals and ourselves to perform complex actions without conscious thought; and if we consider how these can be replicated on a computer, then this could have the following effects on AI research:

▶ New computational tools, techniques and approaches may become available, and these may yield new insights into the classic problems of AI.

▶ New fields of enquiry may be opened up. Many problems that seemed irrelevant to earlier researchers, or simply did not look open to representation on a computer – probably because they involve non-propositional knowledge – might become solvable.

Some commentators have suggested that conventional AI has concentrated only on problems that are amenable to computer solutions – as you learned in Block 1, games like chess are a good example of this – and then labelled the processes required to solve them as 'intelligent' afterwards. A classic circular argument.

The project to bring insights about the mechanisms underlying natural intelligence to difficult computational problems is called **biologically inspired computing**, or often **nouvelle AI**. It is the theme of the rest of the course. Our aim in the remainder of this block is to consider what these mechanisms are – how systematic, ordered, purposeful behaviour can arise without explicit representation – and to offer detailed examples of how they can be applied in real computer systems. The discussion becomes less and less biological as it proceeds, although I will still refer to concepts taken from biology and to examples taken from the natural world.

4.3 A final caution

It may seem that I've been trying to refute or belittle Symbolic AI, to show that it is in some way discredited or simply wrongheaded. This is not so. I do not believe that AI is a failure, or that it is in any way a completed project. It is an ongoing and vital area of research that has had many successes. Like some other areas of technology, it has perhaps become the victim of these successes. Starting with early promise and much hype (most of it not generated by researchers themselves), it has failed to produce sentient androids or superbrains that keep humans as pets, but has moved modestly into the mainstream. Computer systems based on AI principles now reside quietly in washing machines, websites and wireless networks; and AI discoveries have influenced numerous other areas of computing. Predictably, the response has been pretty much that prophesied by the software scientist Bertrand Meyer:

> ... the well-known three-step sequence of reactions that meets the introduction of a new methodological principle: (1) 'it's trivial'; (2) 'besides it won't work'; (3) 'anyway, that's how I did it all along'. (The order may vary.)
>
> Source: Meyer (1997) *Object-oriented Software Construction*, p. 1

Every searcher after new ideas should have a copy of this observation pinned to the head of their bed.

5 | Summary of Unit 1

In this unit I've sought to extend and contrast the conception of intelligence developed in Blocks 1 and 2 by looking at the behaviour of a range of animals. We arrived at an understanding of natural intelligence as, broadly, 'goal-directed, systematic, ordered problem-solving', and considered the meaning of each of these terms. After challenging the conventionally accepted distinctions between natural and artificial entities and between biological and non-biological systems, I then moved on to reflect on the possible influence of a broader understanding of the concept of intelligence on the project of artificial intelligence.

Now look back at the learning outcomes for this unit and check these against what you think you can now do. Return to any section of the unit if you need to.

Unit 2: Mechanisms of natural intelligence

CONTENTS

1	Introduction to Unit 2	42
	What you need to study this unit	42
	Learning outcomes for Unit 2	43
2	Four mechanisms	44
	2.1 Mechanism 1 – interaction	44
	2.2 Mechanism 2 – emergence	57
	2.3 Mechanism 3 – adaptation	63
	2.4 Mechanism 4 – selection	66
3	Summary of Unit 2	70
	References and further reading	167
	Acknowledgements	169
	Index for Block 3	170

Introduction to Unit 2

In Unit 1 we looked at a number of examples of living things behaving in the sort of purposeful, systematic ways that suggest a guiding intelligence of some kind. The question this unit asks is this: how does such behaviour arise in creatures without thought (in any recognisable sense), without logic and language, and with very restricted means of communication? If these animals are not planning, reasoning and designing, as humans do, how is it that they are so deliberate and methodical? What processes are at work?

In this unit I want to suggest *four* mechanisms that can generate purposeful and systematic activity and that can explain the organisation of the ants, the building work of the wasps and the snow goose's sense of direction. Not all of these four are necessarily at work in any one case; singly or in combination, though, they are a group of forces powerful enough to create the most complex and focused behaviour.

Let's start with a rather challenging exercise.

Exercise 2.1

Look back over Case Study 1.6 in the previous unit. Given that the wasps construct their nest collectively, without the benefit of overall management, design or widespread communication, how do you think such a highly structured end-product can arise? I'm not expecting any specialised knowledge: just jot down a few thoughts about this.

Discussion ....

Broadly, I thought the nest seems to result from throwing *large numbers* of agents (individual insects) at the task, probably with some form of *highly localised* communication between them, and with the *whole system* somehow sorting itself out.

In Unit 1 I referred to our characteristically hierarchical, human mode of organising things as top-down. In a bottom-up insect system like this there is no hierarchy and there are no designated sources of authority. All wasps are equal. In the absence of any overall control, then, the results can only be a product of the collective activity of the *whole system*. Every individual does what it does, interacting with its fellows – and the final product somehow materialises.

Let's now look at this idea in more detail. In the rest of the unit I'm going to consider four principles – *interaction*, *emergence*, *adaptation* and *selection* – that seem to underlie the organisation you've seen in the case of the wasps; in the case studies you met in Unit 1; in bottom-up systems in general; and, most broadly, in the strategies all organisms find to survive the trials of life.

What you need to study this unit

You will need the following course components, and will need to use your computer and internet connection for some of the exercises.

▶   this Block 3 text

▶   the course DVD.

LEARNING OUTCOMES FOR UNIT 2

After studying this unit, you will be able to:

2.1 name the four principles from which complex behaviour can arise;

2.2 give examples of how collective behaviour can result from the interactions between a number of simple agents;

2.3 list, with a brief explanation of each, three forms of interaction;

2.4 write a brief explanation of the term 'emergence' and give examples of emergent phenomena in natural and artificial systems;

2.5 explain briefly, with examples, the part that adaptation can play in tuning emergent behaviour in natural and artificial interactive systems;

2.6 write a paragraph explaining the role of selection in evolution.

2 Four mechanisms

2.1 Mechanism 1 – interaction

The word 'interaction' in itself doesn't convey much. Even in the context in which I'm considering it – as a mechanism through which purposeful, 'intelligent' behaviour comes about – it could have several meanings. In this section I'll isolate three ways in which order can arise from interaction: interaction with other agents, interactions with the environment and internal interaction.

Interaction with other agents

We ended the previous section on the question of how organisation can arise in huge colonies of simple creatures such as paper wasps (and the swarm raider ants of Case Study 1.2). It hardly seems likely that any single ant or wasp can be capable of complex planning of any kind, and so there can be no centre of overall control. So how does such ordered behaviour come about?

We can start investigating this question by considering a rather simpler form of collective insect behaviour. In Case Study 1.6 I noted that groups of wasps *forage* for building materials; the army ants of Case Study 1.2 send out pioneers to search for prey. In fact most insect colonies rely on this strategy: members of the group search for food, prey, building materials, etc. and somehow report the location of anything useful they find back to the colony.

Case Study 2.1: Argentine ants and pheromones

Argentine ants (*Linepithema humile*) lay down deposits of special chemicals known as **pheromones** as they move back to their nest after having found a source of food and materials. These deposits are attractive to other ants of the colony, and an individual ant will be impelled to move towards one if it senses it nearby. This phenomenon is known as **recruitment**. In laboratory experiments conducted in 1990, Deneubourg et al. were able to show how this simple means of communication could lead to organised foraging behaviour, using the experimental set-up shown in Figure 2.1.

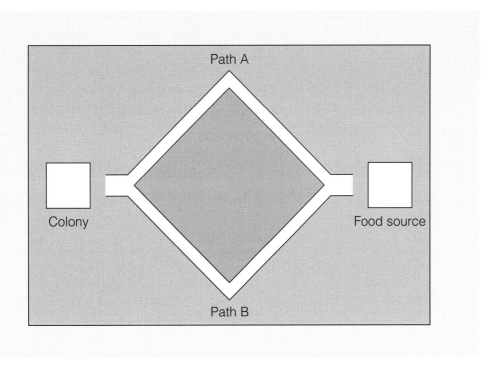

Figure 2.1   Deneubourg's ant foraging experiment (1)

In this version of the experiment, two paths to the food source, A and B, are of equal length. At the start, no ant has any reason to prefer one branch over the other. However, after a while, if a few more ants randomly select, say, Path A then a slightly greater amount of pheromone will be laid down on that branch, which in turn will attract more ants, who will lay down more pheromone. After approximately ten minutes, Deneubourg observed that one branch had become exclusively used and the other left empty. In a variation on the basic experiment, the length of one of the paths was extended to be much longer than the other. In this case, the shortest path was generally selected, since ants returning to the nest had traversed this path twice (from the nest to the source and then back again) and so had laid twice as much pheromone on it. However, the experiment revealed that if the longer path was more than twice the length of the shorter, then in some cases the colony selected the longer path and was unable to break out of this behaviour.

One possible solution to the problem of getting locked into a poor pattern such as this may be to assume that the strength of pheromone trails decays with time. In a computer simulation, which I'll shortly ask you to replicate, Bonabeau et al. (1999) created an initial set-up resembling Figure 2.2 and were able to show that if pheromone evaporation is built into the model, the virtual 'ants' will first exploit the shortest path until the food at the end of it is exhausted, followed by the next shortest, and so on until all sources are finished.

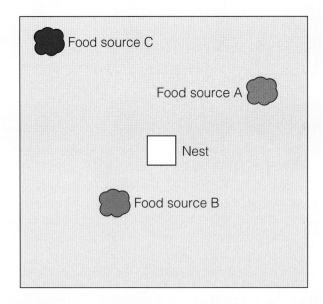

Figure 2.2   Bonabeau's ant foraging simulation

Now, to add some much-needed detail to this picture, we can introduce the computer for the first time. Let's see how much we can learn from Bonabeau's ant colony foraging simulation.

Computer Exercise 2.1

Load Computer Exercise 2.1 from the course DVD and follow the instructions. The results sheet for the exercise is there to help you isolate some of the most important features of the ant system.

Now let's try to derive some of the general principles of this kind of interactive system.

SAQ 2.1

Drawing on the notes you made on the results sheet for Computer Exercise 2.1, note down what features of the ant colony you think enable it to forage effectively. Did any particular properties of the system strike you as interesting or unexpected? What are the properties of a multi-agent interactive system?

ANSWER..

The first point is one that we might have expected. An individual ant on its own is really rather stupid, with only a limited range of stereotyped behaviours at its disposal. In our simulation, without any particular stimulus an ant just wanders around at random. However, the collective behaviour of many of them together becomes purposeful, with no need for leadership or control. The pheromone-based, chemical communication between the ants is necessary for any collective action, but carries only very restricted information and is localised and transient.

We can crystallise the results of the experiment by noting the following key features of our simulated ant colony:

▶ Numerous ants take part in the process.

▶ Every ant has only a very simple set of behaviours.

▶ Therefore, no individual ant has any special status or leadership role.

▶ There is some communication between the ants, but this is very simple ('I've been here'), strictly local (only ants in the vicinity can detect it) and transient (the pheromone may evaporate quite rapidly).

▶ The seemingly organised foraging behaviour builds up over time as a result of many interactions between the ants.

From these specific observations, we can draw up the three main characteristics of an interactive system of the multi-agent type we are examining here:

▶ It is made up of numerous very simple agents, each one capable of a few simple computations and responses.

▶ These agents receive messages or information from other agents nearby, and can send messages back to them, creating feedback loops (recall from Block 1 the importance of feedback to cybernetics).

▶ The behaviour of the whole collective evolves over time.

Since no single agent is in control of the organised activity of the system, we refer to this evolution of systematic behaviour as **self-organisation**.

However, experiments using a set-up similar to Figure 2.3 indicate that in some cases there may be more to it than that. Ants embarking on the longer Path A were observed to be doing U-turns and returning towards the source at round about the point they started to move off at a sharp angle to the right direction, even though the path was well-marked with pheromones. This seemed to indicate that they were not just automatically adjusting to chemical concentrations, but that each ant might carry a memory of previous journeys. In certain circumstances, then, ant behaviour is not chemically determined; ants can make simple decisions. This point will become significant when I come to consider artificial ants.

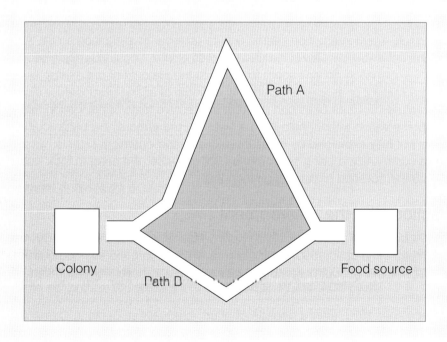

Figure 2.3   Deneubourg's ant foraging experiment (2)

Case Study 2.2: Cockroaches and avoidance behaviour

Nobody likes cockroaches, so the cockroach *Blaberus discoidalis* has become expert at avoiding attack. It is adept at sensing exactly where a threat is coming from and taking swift evasive action in the safest direction. The mechanisms of cockroach avoidance behaviour have been studied in detail and are now reasonably well understood. A cockroach senses an impending attack by means of two structures on the rear of its abdomen, known as 'cerci', which are covered with hairs sensitive to the strength and direction of air currents. However, the cerci are tuned to distinguish between genuine attacks and mere breezes: they only become active when the air over the hairs is accelerating at more than 0.6 m s^{-2} (metres per second per second). They also extract directional information from the flow of air (rather as the lobster we met in Case Study 1.5 discovers directions from odour plumes). The insect does not respond in any way to the movements of other cockroaches.

As soon as its cerci detect threatening activity, the cockroach immediately begins avoidance behaviour. Within 58 milliseconds, if it is standing still at the time of the attack, or within 14 milliseconds if it is already moving, it begins a turn, taking about 20–30 milliseconds. The angle of the turn is not random, but based on the direction of the wind, local obstacles and the direction of the light, if any. On completing the turn, the insect moves rapidly in the selected direction.

Case Study 2.3: Honeybees and food location

Honeybees (*Apis mellifera*) are foraging insects that are able to navigate around their neighbourhood and form maps of the territory around their nests. It is well known that foraging worker bees have a system of signalling the sites of food discoveries to other members of the colony. Exactly how bees manage such feats in unpredictable conditions – where food sources may come and go, where celestial guides such as the sun are often covered by cloud, and where local landmarks may be hidden – is still the subject of argument. Most of the evidence points to the hypothesis that bees use a combination of dead reckoning, navigation by landmarks and the sun, and systematic search (in situations in which there are no cues available at all).

Figure 2.5   The honeybee, doing what it does best

There are competing theories of how bees, with their very limited brains, are able to steer using landmarks. One is that foragers leaving the hive memorise a 'home vector' based on the average of the main features of the landscape around them – mountains, houses, and so on. As they fly back to the hive from the food source they constantly recalculate and fly along a vector based on these landmarks as they appear from their current position, always flying in such a direction as to reduce the difference between their present vector and the initial, 'home' vector.

There is also good experimental evidence that bees only activate memories that apply to the particular situation they are in. For instance, a bee returning to the hive will activate its memory of the home vector and landmarks; on the other hand, one that is just leaving the hive to forage will use a different set of memories, temporarily discarding others.

A word of caution here. When I claim that the bee is 'calculating a vector', I certainly don't mean that it is explicitly doing linear algebra in its head. A bee wouldn't be capable of anything of the sort. But remember my comment in Unit 1: when you catch a ball, your nervous system is doing complex real-time calculations – you just aren't aware of it. The same could be said of the bee.

Exercise 2.2

Think back to our earlier discussion of Ambler. What differences can you see between the way the cockroach and the bee cope with the world and the way Ambler did? What do you think makes the two insects so good at it, and Ambler so poor?

Discussion ....

Ambler's problem was, as Kelly pointed out, that after every movement it had to stop to think. At each step, Ambler sensed where it was, compared it with its symbolic mental map, sorted through alternatives for its next step, weighed up the pros and cons of each, made a decision and then acted. No wonder its brain had to be so big it couldn't be carried on board.

The insect cases, I think, suggest two vital differences. Firstly, each individual has *no* complete, symbolic internal map of its environment. At all times, it relies heavily and continuously on a few features it senses in the environment itself. Secondly, each has only a very restricted set of behaviours available at any one time. Neither creature needs to weigh alternatives for its next action. It simply *acts*.

We can sum up these two crucial differences in slightly more formal terms. There are two features of the insect systems that weren't present in Ambler:

▶ **Parsimony**. There are no complex internal representations, and almost certainly no symbols of any kind. The cockroach may generate some internal information about the strength and direction of an impending attack when required, but this can't be coded in any explicit form: there simply isn't the internal complexity to achieve this. The same is true of the bee: it 'remembers' certain basic information about the location of its hive, possibly as a crude two-dimensional picture, but that is all. In both cases, the insect only carries the bare minimum of information it needs to function in a particular situation.

▶ **Fluent coupling**. In both insect examples, the creature isn't taking periodic measurements and then pausing while it performs complicated internal processing on them, so it can decide what to do next – as Ambler had to do. Instead, what we are seeing is the insect's sensory apparatus, the muscles which move its body, and the environment all working together as a closely coupled system.

You may remember that Shakey and other examples of conventional robots performed their routines in exceptionally simplistic environments, containing only a few geometrically regular objects, perhaps, and with carefully controlled lighting and neutrally painted walls. It should now be obvious why. The complexities of the jumbled, dynamic and perpetually surprising world we (and our insect friends) inhabit are simply impossible to represent in an internal symbolic model. And, as our discussion of the Frame Problem in Block 2 showed, it quickly overwhelms any attempt to reason about it.

At this point, it is useful to consider a fresh aspect of the kind of tight coupling between an organism and its environment that we are talking about here. You may recall that earlier I mentioned in passing the fact that paper wasps do not communicate using pheromones, in the way ants do. Yet somehow they manage to collaborate in large, highly organised groups. Consider this question.

Exercise 2.3

It seems clear that, for the sort of organisation that paper wasps manage, some form of communication must be going on among them. Can you think of any way they might communicate so as to coordinate their building activities, if they have no explicit signalling system?

Discussion ....

If we accept that the wasps have no proto-language like bee dances or pheromone trails, there is only one possibility. The insects communicate with one another *through the environment*. One insect modifies the environment in a certain way and another then senses and responds to this change. This concept is known as **stigmergy**.

Foraging bees returning to their nests are observed to carry out elaborate 'dances', in which the movements of their bodies communicate the distance and direction of pollen sources to other workers.

It appears, then, that simple creatures like insects are not only themselves tightly coupled with their environment, in some cases they are also tightly coupled with one another via the environment. In fact, the laying of pheromone trails can be seen as a form of stigmergy, since by depositing chemicals an insect is modifying its environment, but the term is usually taken to mean a more indirect form of interaction. Stigmergy is now a key concept in experimental research in robotics, multi-agent systems and communication in computer networks, and will play an important part in later discussions.

So this, then, is our second kind of interaction. You may recall that in Block 1 I stressed the immense significance of the concepts of *embodiment* and *situatedness* to modern ideas in artificial intelligence – the crucial insight that animals are *active*, moving through the world and constantly engaging with it. I re-emphasise the point here. In 1995, the philosopher Andy Clark offered an elegant summary of this insight:

> ... our minds ... are organs for rapidly initiating the next move in real-world situations. They are organs exquisitely geared to the production of actions, laid out in local space and real time. Once mind is cast as a controller of bodily actions, layers upon layers of once-received wisdom fall away. The distinction between perception and cognition, the idea of executive control centres in the brain, and a widespread vision of rationality itself are all called into question.

> Source: Clark (1995)

Let's now consider some further points about bodies and embodiment.

Internal interaction

So far our discussion has centred on comparatively simple creatures, such as insects. Interacting with each other in swarms or alone (only a minority of insects are social) and coupled with their environment, they show goal-directed, systematic behaviour, sometimes with intricate results: webs, honeycombs, castles and other structures. But what about more obviously complex and evolved creatures such as birds, beavers, apes or, indeed, humans? Surely it would be fanciful to suggest that their behaviour can simply be the result of interactions between senses, muscles and surroundings. Intelligence has to be more than sets of mechanical reflexes. It has to be more than a dynamic coupling with the environment. Surely it is obvious that in any but the most basic creatures something extra is going on *inside*? But what?

Of course, there is plenty of justice in this objection and I'll try to answer it shortly. But first, let's raise one question.

Exercise 2.4

The word 'simple' came up time and time again in the discussion of my insect case studies. Generally, what do you think the word 'simple' was intended to mean in these contexts?

Discussion ....

I seem to have used the word 'simple' to refer to two classes of thing. Firstly, to the creatures themselves. I've often called them 'simple' – roughly meaning 'not complicated', 'easy to understand' or perhaps 'not made up of many parts'. Secondly, I often referred to insect behaviours as 'simple', by which I meant 'not hard to do' or 'not requiring intelligence'.

But the line of thought leading to the question I started this subsection with may contain two mistaken assumptions, both of which centre on that troublesome word 'simple':

▶ that animals such as insects are 'simple' (whatever 'simple' may mean here);

▶ that actions such as standing and walking, recognising and manipulating objects, moving from A to B and navigating around a world of objects are too 'simple' to require intelligence. After all, we perform them without apparent thought, and they seem to cause even insects no trouble, so surely they must just be a matter of straightforward mechanics?

Your reading of Block 2 will have at least taught you the error of the second assumption. Object recognition, robotic locomotion and planning are among the areas where AI has been least effective and convincing. In dismissing them as 'simple' – beneath the notice of artificial intelligence – we are overlooking tasks of amazing complexity, most of which are ill understood. As I pointed out in Unit 1 of this block, many human abilities seem to involve exactly this sort of non-propositional knowledge. Every minute of every day, we carry out all kinds of actions without conscious thought and then dub them 'simple' – but they simply are not.

In fact, both these assumptions could be just plain wrong. 'Simple' creatures are not necessarily that simple. 'Simple' actions which we take for granted often require immensely complex systems to produce them. Inside even the humblest creatures are intricate webs of interactions out of which actions arise. Let's look at an example.

Case Study 2.4: Insect walking
So you think walking is easy?

In our studies of insect foraging and building, I took it for granted that walking was something that insects just *did*. It's something we 'just do' ourselves. I didn't pause to consider what an astounding accomplishment walking is, in insect or human. Even walking on an unobstructed flat plane is a remarkable feat of organisation, balance and coordination. And if we take into account common factors, such as roughness of ground, obstacles, slopes, lateral pressures (e.g. wind pressure), the need to move at different speeds, and so on, taking a simple walk adds up to a truly formidable task.

Insects are much easier to study than most other animals, and six legs can be a big advantage in unpredictable terrain, so the hexapodal (six-legged) gait of creatures such as cockroaches has been intensively investigated. As the insect moves, each leg has two basic phases:

▶ *swing* (the leg is lifted and moves forward)

▶ *stance* (the leg is grounded, providing support and pushing the body forward).

The aim of any gait is to provide firm support for the insect's body at all times, while moving it forward. Insects use a different gait according to the speed at which they want to travel; but at all times legs in the stance phase should form a polygon, with the centre of gravity of the body inside it (see Figure 2.6). At low speeds, only one leg swings at a time in a pattern known as a **metachronal wave**. However, as it moves faster, the insect switches to the tripod pattern shown in Figure 2.6. In all cases, the sequence of leg swings starts at the back and moves forward, in a wave-like pattern.

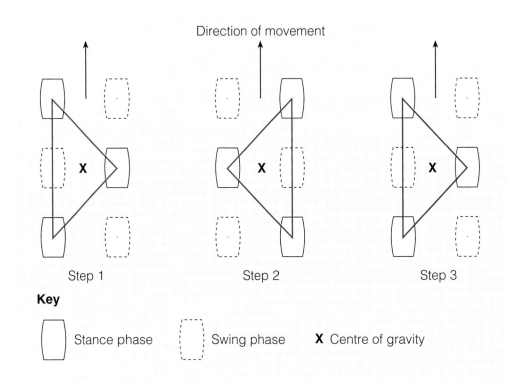

Figure 2.6   Insect walking – tripodal gait, during three steps

At first sight, you might guess that some central controller in the insect's brain must send signals to the legs and coordinate their activity. Repeated experiments have shown that this idea is false. Insect brains are tiny or non-existent. In real insects, there is no evidence of any central controller. Instead, management of each leg seems to rest with the leg itself. Each leg has its own controller, and walking is achieved purely through *interactions* between these internal controllers.

Consider Figure 2.7, a much simplified model of how this is thought to work. Each leg is pictured as being moved by a separate controller. Each controller is responsible for moving its leg forward (swing), planting it firmly and pushing it backwards (stance). The legs are coordinated by means of the signals the leg controllers send to one another – I've represented them as numbers 1, 2 and 3 on the diagram.

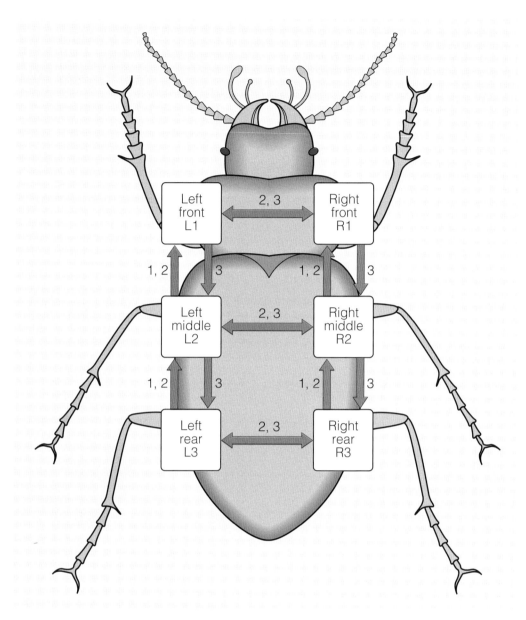

Figure 2.7   Insect walking – internal interaction model

Let's just isolate one controller, the right front (R1), and consider how it behaves. It gets four signals from other leg controllers, 1 and 2 from the right middle and 2 and 3 from the left front.

▶ Signal 1 from R2 restrains R1 from starting its swing until R2 is in its stance and supporting the body.

▶ Signal 2 from R2 and L1 stimulates R1 to begin its swing just as these two legs begin their power strokes.

▶ Signal 3 from L1 stimulates R1 to start its swing while L1 is in stance phase.

The timing of these signals is finely tuned (although not centrally coordinated) to produce the metachronal wave and the smooth, effortless gait of the insect in a variety of conditions. We'll look at a robotic model of the process in Unit 4 of this block.

This, then, is our third and final type of interaction: the complex interplay between internal units inside a living creature that gives rise to behaviour. But what exactly are these units? We have looked at a simplified model of an insect in which motor modules interact, but how are they realised in actual living insects? I'll try to offer a fuller answer to this question in Unit 4, but we can anticipate the discussion briefly before we move on.

Exercise 2.5

In general, what sort of mechanisms do you think make up the walking system of real insects, modelled above? What, if anything, do you already know about such constituents?

Discussion ....

You might have noted something along the following lines: in all but the simplest of creatures (amoebae, plants, and so on), internal interactions take place in a *nervous system*, made up of webs of interconnecting nerve cells. This is a fact the cyberneticists knew. Specialised **neurons** make up the sensory system of every animal, while other specialised neurons activate the muscles.

In real insects, the separate interacting modules of the walking model we met above are made up of hundreds of nerve cells, densely connected and interacting with one another through excitatory and inhibitory signals.

The whole of Block 4 is devoted to a study of the properties and applications of computer models of nervous systems. I've said enough on the subject for now. Let's move to a brief summary of interaction.

Summary of interaction

It might be useful at this point for you to have a quick look back over the last few pages. I've discussed three types of interaction. To help you sum these up in your own mind, think about the following question.

SAQ 2.4

What are the three types of interaction that have been described? Give a brief definition, using your own words, of each one and recall one example of each.

ANSWER...

The three types of interaction are:

▶ *Multi-agent interaction.* Many simple agents collaborate on a problem, but there is no central control of their collaboration. Organised behaviour arises from simple local communications between the agents. I offered the example of social insects communicating by means of pheromones when foraging or building.

▶ *Environmental interaction.* An organism produces systematic behaviour by continuous and immediate reaction to information it senses in its environment. There is no 'thought' or 'deliberation' between sensing and acting. My examples were bee navigation by reference to landmarks and cockroach avoidance behaviour.

▶ *Internal interaction.* This occurs in nearly all organisms. Behaviour comes from the interaction between specialised modules, themselves comprising dense webs of communicating neurons. I illustrated this with a discussion of a very simplified model of insect walking.

I've spent quite a lot of time discussing interaction because it is the foundation of the other three mechanisms outlined in this unit. Without interaction, emergence could not happen and adaptation and selection would not work. We can now move on to look at these three mechanisms.

2.2 | Mechanism 2 – emergence

Let's now turn to the second of the four mechanisms underlying natural intelligence – emergence. Rather than start with a definition of this rather difficult concept, first I want you to look at a classic computer simulation. This should give you an intuitive grasp of the idea of emergence in certain types of complex systems.

Computer Exercise 2.3

Complete Computer Exercise 2.3, 'The Game of Life', on the course DVD.

The Game of Life belongs to a large class of computer systems known as **cellular automata**. These have been much studied and are used to investigate a range of issues in science and the social sciences. When you've completed the exercise, consider this question.

SAQ 2.5

How closely does The Game of Life system conform to our earlier definition of a multi-agent interactive system?

ANSWER...

All of the following features of the kinds of interactive systems you studied in the previous section are also features of The Game of Life:

▶ The systems contain numerous simple agents.

▶ These agents have limited, regional knowledge of one another.

▶ They are feedback systems – changes in step n of the evolution of the system will affect step $n + 1$.

▶ In certain cases, they show complex behaviour evolving over time.

Before moving on, it's worth highlighting one further feature of The Game of Life.

SAQ 2.6

Did you notice any distinctive feature of the way in which the simulation evolves from its starting point? How much does the exact starting pattern matter?

ANSWER...

The way the simulation evolves appears to be very sensitive to the exact nature of the starting state: that is, to the initial pattern of live and dead cells on the grid. Many start states lead immediately either to nothing at all, a grid of dead cells, or to some boring equilibrium state (such as a block or oscillating pattern), after which nothing else happens. However, others lead to interesting, evolving patterns, which seem complex and unpredictable.

So the behaviour of many multi-agent interactive systems will be very sensitive to their starting state, as well as to other parameters.

Let's now take a rather deeper look at The Game of Life.

Computer Exercise 2.4

Complete Computer Exercise 2.4 on the course DVD.

Exercise 2.6

What structures did you observe during the evolution of the simulation? Could these be classified into types?

Discussion ....

The Game of Life seems to be capable of generating a huge variety of patterns. Among these are:

▶ stable structures such as **blocks**;

▶ oscillating structures or **blinkers**;

▶ patterns that move across the grid, reconstituting themselves after a certain fixed number of steps – the best known of these is called a **glider**;

▶ structures which regularly generate other structures, such as **glider guns**, which periodically emit a new glider;

▶ **eaters** – configurations that destroy other patterns such as gliders that collide with them.

The Cambridge mathematician, John Conway, who invented The Game of Life, was able to arrange glider guns and eaters to form logic gates (AND, OR, NOT, etc.), and connect them into complicated switching circuits. He showed that these circuits could then be organised into a Universal Turing Machine – a general-purpose computer of the form discussed in Block 1, capable of computing any function expressible in algorithmic form. And such a 'computer' has indeed been built.

Now we can introduce the idea of **emergence**. We can state that structures (gliders, blocks, puffer-trains, beehives, etc.) of The Game of Life *emerge* from interactions (the rules of birth and death) between simple components (individual cells).

Exercise 2.7

Take some of the examples discussed in Section 2.1. In each case, identify the emergent property or behaviour and the low-level interactions from which it arises.

Discussion ....

In the case of insect colonies, for example, the emergent behaviour is the foraging pattern or nest-building activity, and the low-level interactions are between insects via pheromone trails. In the insect-walking case study, the emergent properties are the particular gaits the animal or robot adopts; the low-level interactions are between the leg controllers and between the more basic units that make them up.

We can make the following general points about the properties of structures or behaviours that emerge from low-level interactions:

▶ They are ordered patterns that persist over time.

▶ The patterns may be physical and enduring, as in the case of wasps' nests; or they may be transient patterns such as ant columns, which are formed from elements of the medium itself (in this case, the ants).

▶ The same set of low-level interactions and rules may support many different stable states: The Game of Life, as you've seen, allows a multitude of different stable patterns.

▶ Emergent systems are likely to go through **bifurcations** as they evolve: there will be abrupt changes of behaviour. For example, you saw in Case Study 1.6 that some event causes the wasps suddenly to stop building a comb and start on an envelope around it.

What is emergence?

You can probably already see that this is a hard question. A full discussion of it might take us deeper into philosophical issues than I really want to go. However, emergence is now such an important idea in modern science, computing and philosophy that I think it is worth spending a bit of time thinking about it here.

Emergence seems to have something to do with the *whole* in a complex system, composed of interacting components, being in some way *more* than the sum of these *parts*. But what can the word 'more' mean here? An early attempt at an answer came from the English philosopher, John Stuart Mill (1806–1873). Mill distinguished between what he called **homeopathic** and **heteropathic effects** in complex systems. A homeopathic effect is simply the sum of effects of each of the parts of the system acting individually. For example, in a system consisting of three connected motors, all turning in the same direction with torque t_1, t_2 and t_3, the overall torque (the homeopathic effect) will simply be $t_1 + t_2 + t_3$. However, Mill argued that *heteropathic* effects cannot be understood in this way: the outcome is more than just the sum of the effects of the parts, and can only be explained in terms of certain supplementary **heteropathic laws**, which he described as 'laws of combined agency [which] are not compounded of the laws of the separate agencies'. Mill offered an example of a heteropathic effect in the chemical reaction:

$$NaOH + HCl \rightarrow NaCl + H_2O$$

or in words,

sodium hydroxide plus hydrochloric acid gives sodium chloride plus water

The product of the reaction, water and a salt, is in no sense the sum of the effects of the initial reactants, an acid and a base.

Emergence and reduction

Most scientific explanations are **reductive**: they account for phenomena wholly in terms of simpler things. For instance, the behaviour of a volume of gas can be fully explained in terms of the random movements of the trillions of molecules that make it up. The gas laws can be *reduced* to the statistical effects of interactions between innumerable small particles. But emergence seems to be rather more than this. We might want to contrast the reduction of X to Y with the emergence of X from Y as follows:

▶ in the case of the reduction of X to Y, X is held to be *nothing* but Y;

▶ in the case of the emergence of X from Y, X is somehow *more* than Y.

So emergent phenomena cannot be fully reduced to the properties and activities of the lower-level domain.

Modern thinkers are now inclined to see emergence as the appearance of some (high-level) phenomenon – an entity, property, law or process – out of the activity of more fundamental (low-level) phenomena. However, to be truly emergent, this new phenomenon must be in some way 'novel' or 'unexpected', in some sense irreducible to the activity of the lower level base from which it arose. The philosopher David Chalmers suggests the following definition of emergence:

> Emergence is the phenomenon wherein complex, interesting high-level function is produced as a result of combining simple low-level mechanisms in simple ways ... [it] is the phenomenon wherein a system is designed according to certain principles, but interesting properties arise that are not included in the goals of the designer.
>
> Source: Chalmers (2002) *Varieties of Emergence*, p. 1

The emergent properties are not properties of the individual parts of the low-level domain. You can see that such an idea describes the behaviour of, say, insect colonies very well. It is hard to believe that one could *deduce* that structured nests and organised foraging would arise just from a description of the behaviour of individual insects: one has to put insects together and watch the processes unfold.

One recent account of such a layered conception of nature can be found in Morowitz (2002).

In general, then, emergence involves some sort of relation between phenomena belonging to a low-level (or fundamental) domain and phenomena belonging to a high-level (or derivative) domain. All this suggests a *layered* conception of the world: nature is structured as a series of levels – physical, chemical, biological, psychological, social, etc. Each layer embodies properties and laws that are emergent from the layer below and not fully reducible to it. This idea of layering is, of course, already very familiar to computer scientists.

Strong and weak emergence

If an emergent phenomenon is more than the sum of the parts that give rise to it and cannot be fully explained by, or reduced to, these parts, then to what extent is this phenomenon something genuinely *new*, truly a thing in its own right?

Some theorists make a distinction between **strong** and **weak emergence**. Chalmers suggests that a high-level phenomenon is strongly emergent from a low-level domain when we could never deduce facts about the phenomenon from facts about the low-level domain – even if we knew *everything* about the low-level domain and had god-like powers of reasoning. Strongly emergent phenomena simply cannot be predicted from knowledge of their low-level base: they are something radically new and different. By contrast, a high-level phenomenon is weakly emergent from a low-level domain when facts about that phenomenon are *unexpected*, but could in principle be deduced from facts about the low-level domain, given enough knowledge, time and reasoning power. Strongly emergent phenomena are entities in their own right, with properties and powers that are theirs alone and in no way those of the low-level domains that give rise to them. Weakly emergent phenomena are just interesting and novel aspects, or products, of the lower-level domain.

The whole issue of the real existence of emergent phenomena, independent of the low-level domains that give rise to them, is deeply controversial. Are there, in fact, *any* instances of strongly emergent phenomena in nature, emergent entities with properties and powers of their own? Consider this very difficult question.

Exercise 2.8

Do you think there are any phenomena in nature that are strongly emergent? You can draw on your own knowledge or, if you like, look back at some of the examples and case studies in this, and earlier, units. Don't be troubled if you don't get too far with the question.

Discussion ....

It is very hard to think of any. Many theorists believe that there are *no* strongly emergent phenomena; that strong emergence is inconsistent with materialism and scientifically irrelevant. The entangled states found in quantum mechanics have been suggested as candidates for strong emergence. Chalmers maintains that there is at least one 'clear' case of a strongly emergent phenomenon and that is *consciousness*. But I think both these suggestions are dubious.

Weak emergence is a far less controversial issue, although, as might be expected, there has been plenty of controversy about what the term actually means. Chalmers suggests that '*emergence is a psychological property*, rather than a thing in its own right'. Properties can be called emergent if they fulfil both of the following:

▶ They are interesting to a given observer.

▶ It is difficult for the observer to deduce the property from the low-level interactions that give rise to it.

Other theorists concur. Emmerich, for instance, says, '... the important aspect of emergent events ... lies not in the simulations themselves, but in the fact that they change the way we think about the world. Rather than being emergent arrangements *in themselves* ... simulations [are] able to set off emergent processes in our own minds'.

But there is one obvious problem with this understanding of weak emergence as something 'novel' or 'unexpected'. Andy Clark has pointed out that:

> sometimes the general notion of emergence is equated with the idea of unexpected behaviours ... The trouble here is that what is unexpected to one person may be just what someone else predicts ... What we really need, then, is an observer-independent criterion ...
>
> Source: Clark (1997)

I will have to leave the discussion there.

Emergence in artificial systems

Obviously, this is all very abstract, difficult and seemingly removed from the purposes of M366. Let's return to our main concern – understanding and building biologically inspired systems capable of some form of intelligence. For this, we can adopt a conception of emergence due to Holland (1998). He maintains that it is possible to reduce the behaviour of a whole to the lawful behaviour of its parts if we take the **non-linear** interactions into account. According to this view:

See the course Maths Guide for a definition of non-linear.

▶ Emergence occurs in systems that are generated. The systems are composed of copies of a relatively small number of components that obey simple laws.

▶ The whole is more than the sum of the parts in these generated systems. Interactions between the parts are non-linear, so the overall behaviour cannot be obtained by summing the behaviour of the individual components.

▶ Emergent phenomena in generated systems are, typically, persistent patterns with changing components.

▶ The context of a persistent emergent pattern determines its function. For example, one could make different uses of a 'glider' in interactions with other local structures in The Game of Life.

▶ Interactions between persistent patterns provide increasing 'competence' as the number of such patterns increases. The number of possible interactions, and hence the possible sophistication of response, rises rapidly as the number of interacting components in the system grows.

▶ Persistent patterns often satisfy macro-laws. The law describing the movement of a 'glider' in The Game of Life is a clear example.

▶ Differential persistence is a typical consequence of the laws that generate emergent phenomena. This applies mainly to evolutionary systems. In these, structures that persist long enough to produce copies are the ones that generate new variants. This should become clearer later in this unit and in Block 5.

Now let's wrap up this section with a question and an exercise.

SAQ 2.7

Write a brief definition of the term 'emergence'.

ANSWER..

Given what we have learned up to this point, it might be hard for you to come up with anything succinct. Perhaps you might have written something like 'the appearance of novel and/or unpredictable, regular patterns or laws arising in systems from interactions between their simple, low-level components'. This is a good enough working definition, I think, although there are some questions. Just how important is novelty or unpredictability? Is the real issue whether patterns can be deduced at all, as in the case of strong emergence? Also, this definition downplays the importance of initial (and other external) conditions, yet these cannot be ruled out completely.

But, despite all this complication, it is necessary to talk about emergence and come to some sort of understanding of it. Emergence is a very widespread phenomenon in the natural and human worlds; and it has recently become a key talking point in science and computing. All of the biological structures and behaviours we've discussed in this and the previous unit are weakly emergent phenomena. They arise from the constituent parts of lower-level systems and are generated by simple interactions between those parts over time. All the artificial systems I'll be considering in later units rely on weak emergence.

Finally, let's consider a last case of emergence, this time in the social, rather than the biological, domain. Then we can move on to consider the third of our four principles – adaptation.

Computer Exercise 2.5 (optional)

Complete Computer Exercise 2.5 on the course DVD.

Exercise 2.9

Try to think of two or three other emergent properties or behaviours that are commonly encountered.

Discussion ....

The behaviour of stock markets and the World Wide Web might be good examples. For example, the number of links to web pages seems to be governed by mathematical laws, despite there being no overall control.

2.3 | Mechanism 3 – adaptation

So far, we have considered how complex interactions between numerous units, modules or agents, internal and external, can lead to the emergence of unexpected, systematic and useful behaviour – behaviour we might perhaps be inclined to label as in some way 'intelligent'. But if we really want to talk about intelligence in real animals in their natural environment, evidently something vital is missing from the analysis so far. To try and make this a bit clearer, consider the following.

Case Study 2.5: Sphex wasps and food provision

The female sphex wasp (*Sphex cognatus*) digs a burrow in which to lay her eggs, abandoning them to hatch on their own. However, before leaving she provides a source of fresh food for the hatched grubs by stinging and paralysing a large insect, such as a moth or cricket, and leaving it in the burrow next to the eggs. The wasp drags the immobilised prey to the mouth of the burrow, leaves it on the ground just outside and then goes down into the burrow, apparently to check for predators that might be hiding inside. If the burrow is safe, she then comes up and drags the prey inside, leaving it close to the eggs. This looks like systematic and purposeful behaviour.

However, if an experimenter is present and moves the prey a short distance from the burrow entrance while the wasp is inside, when she re-emerges she will drag the cricket *back* to its original position at the mouth of the entrance, and then go down into the burrow again to check. And if the experimenter then moves the prey again, the same pattern will be repeated. The cycle can go on until the insect dies of exhaustion.

SAQ 2.8

What do you think is happening here? Why does the insect respond in this way?

ANSWER..

It seems fairly clear that what looks to us like an intelligent piece of planning and forethought, is really just a piece of instinctive unvarying behaviour. In much the same way that a crude industrial robot would go on welding or spraying, even if there was no car in front of it on the production line, so the wasp has no means of adapting its choice of actions to changed circumstances. Like the automata of Block 1, her behaviour is hard-wired.

In a way, our reaction to the wasp's actions is just a case of Clever Hans all over again – another example of anthropomorphism. Behaviour which seems to us remarkably intelligent simply isn't. In fact, here the wasp's actions are hardly any smarter than those of a clock or a thermostat. However, the moral I want to draw from this story is a slightly different one. It is this: for true intelligence, systematic, goal-directed behaviour is not enough on its own. Genuinely intelligent behaviour must also be *flexible*, a point you may remember we made in Unit 1, Section 3.3. Intelligent creatures are aware of changes in their environment and are able to adjust what they are doing in response. They have to be *adaptable*.

Creatures or species with absolutely fixed behaviour patterns are sure to be extinguished in the long run, because they inhabit a challenging and ever-changing world. Sooner or later, events will conspire to crush them. But nature seems to have allowed for this: as the world changes, we observe that the living things that inhabit it change too. We call this **adaptation**.

brittle – when confronted with inputs for which they have never been programmed they simply collapse. Although there has always been some interest in the AI community in machine learning, it has never been a major pursuit.

Now let's sum up what you've learned about learning.

Exercise 2.12

Write down a brief definition of learning that will cover the sorts of cases we discussed above.

Discussion ....

Of course you could find various possibilities in the dictionaries. One possible definition that might cover the cases we've considered would run something like 'The process by which relatively permanent changes occur in behavioural potential as a result of experience' (John Anderson in *Learning and Memory: An integrated approach*); or 'changes in an individual's behaviour arising from experience; a relatively permanent change in cognition, resulting from experience and directly influencing behaviour'.

The key appears to be the effect of experience on behaviour. But all this must seem unsatisfactory as an account of *human* learning, There is no doubt that humans can learn by conditioning; but our experience feeds into and modifies an immense pool of knowledge, concepts, plans, cognitive frameworks, presuppositions, and so on – all of which shape our behaviour, now and in the future. Higher animals like chimps also have sophisticated mental structures that are modified by learning.

2.4 Mechanism 4 – selection

In the previous section, we distinguished between two types of adaptation:

▶ adaptation of the individual over its lifetime

▶ adaptation of the species over several generations.

We discussed the first of these, reserving for it the term *adaptation*. In this section I want to look at the second kind of adaptation – alteration of an entire species over many generations in response to changes in the environment.

Let's start with another very well-known case study.

Case Study 2.6: Peppered moths and camouflage

In 1848 the population of English peppered moths (*Biston betularia*) around Manchester was characteristically light coloured, with a dappled surface to the wings. However, there was a rare dark variant, which comprised about 2% of the moth population. By 1898 the area had become highly industrialised and naturalists were observing that the vast majority of moths appeared to have lost their flecked appearance and become dark in colour.

Figure 2.8   English peppered Moths (light and dark variants)

Exercise 2.13

What do you think happened here? One of the keys to the puzzle is the dates and the location where this took place.

Discussion ....

The entomologist J. W. Tutt suggested an explanation in 1895, which was generally supported by field experiments conducted by Bernard Kettlewell in the 1950s. The years 1848 to 1898 were a period of rapid industrialisation. Numerous factories had opened up in the area, with chimneys belching out clouds of soot and dark smoke, which coated trees, buildings and every other surface. Both moth variants were extremely appetising to the wide variety of birds that preyed on them, but in 1848 the normal moth had an excellent answer to its enemies: its peppered colouring made it almost impossible to see against the background of lichens and mosses that then covered trees and buildings; the dark variants were easily picked out and eaten by the sharp-eyed birds. However, by 1898, the layers of grime on every surface meant that it was the dark variety that was now difficult to spot, whereas its peppered fellows stood out like Pinocchio's nose and were quickly eaten. Compare Figures 2.8 and 2.9.

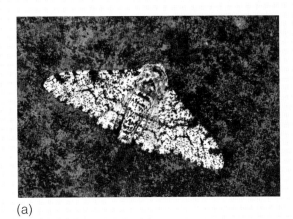 

(a)   (b)

Figure 2.9   English peppered moths against darker backgrounds.

It's fair to say that there has been some recent controversy over the significance and interpretation of the case of the peppered moth (and much distortion). Most biologists, however, believe that Tutt's explanation of the phenomenon still stands. Before we discuss the implications of this, there are one or two details to fill in:

▶ No individual moth changed its colour. No moth could 'decide' that the world had become dark and so it was time to become dark. No individual could make such adaptations in its lifetime: if you were born dark, you stayed dark.

▶ However, there was an inbuilt and fairly constant variation in the entire population of moths: in 1848 about 2% of them were born dark (and stayed dark). We now know that this was the result of a mutation.

▶ The offspring of dark moths would be dark, while the offspring of normal peppered moths would be light and peppered.

▶ In 1848 very few of the dark moths were surviving to have any offspring. They were being gobbled up before they could mate, with only a few lucky individuals managing to escape being eaten long enough to produce dark offspring.

▶ In 1898, it was the light peppered moths that were failing to reproduce. The dark variants were thriving in their new sooty world and producing many generations of dark offspring.

You can investigate the mechanics of this phenomenon more fully through a computer simulation.

Computer Exercise 2.6

Complete Computer Exercise 2.6 on the course DVD.

This mechanism we see at work here – **natural selection** – is now well known and will forever be associated with the name of Charles Darwin (1809–1882).

Darwin (1859) observed that every species produces far more offspring than are needed to keep its population steady – one pair of houseflies, for example, might have as many as 100 000 offspring over the course of an average life. Clearly, unless some force limited their numbers, the whole Earth would have long ago been covered by flies. But, as we all know, such forces do exist – every living thing inhabits an uncertain and dangerous world, one with only limited resources: organisms are preyed upon; they succumb to accident and illness; they starve to death when food is scarce; they struggle among themselves to find mates. There are countless pressures acting on creatures, continuously cutting their numbers. Darwin called this the 'struggle for existence'. His great contribution was to put together the following chain of reasoning:

Figure 2.10 Charles Darwin

1   Living organisms have more offspring than the environment could possibly support.

2   Members of a species struggle among themselves, and with other species, for the limited resources available in their environment.

3   Organisms vary.

4   The variants that are best equipped for the struggle survive long enough to reproduce and pass on their advantageous features to the next generation; less well-adapted variants die before they can reproduce.

5   Thus, species gradually adapt to their environmental conditions.

Summing up the results of all this in his classic work, *On the Origin of Species*, Darwin wrote:

> It may be said that natural selection is daily and hourly scrutinising, throughout the world, every variation, even the slightest; rejecting that which is bad, preserving and adding up all that is good; silently and insensibly working ... at the improvement of each organic being in relation to its organic and inorganic conditions of life.

> Source: Darwin (1859) *On the Origin of Species*, Chapter 4

Notice that this is quite different from the sort of adaptation we were discussing in the previous section. Darwin goes on:

> We see nothing of these slow changes in progress, until the hand of time has marked the long lapses of ages, and then so imperfect is our view into long past geological ages, that we only see that the forms of life are now different from what they formerly were.

> Source: Darwin (1859) *On the Origin of Species*, Chapter 4

Again, you may now wonder what this can have to do with computing. Surely evolution by natural selection is a *biological* process operating on living organisms in the natural world? Computing has to do with the mechanistic working of algorithms on data structures inside the closed world of the computer. But **evolutionary computation** – that is, a form of computing inspired by the key ideas of Darwinian natural selection – is a major strand of twenty-first century computing theory and practice. I'll look at an example of evolutionary computation in Unit 4 of this block, and the whole of Block 5 is devoted to the subject.

3 Summary of Unit 2

Let's now review what you have learned in this unit. We have discussed four mechanisms through which the systematic, purposeful behaviour with ordered outcomes that we see all around us in nature can arise in creatures without logic, language or conscious reasoning.

SAQ 2.10

Write a sentence or two, in note form, summing up what you understand by each of the following four terms: interaction, emergence, adaptation and selection.

ANSWER..

Here is what I might have written by way of a summary of the points that have come up in the unit.

▶ *Interaction*. A mechanism in which communication between a number of units results in a complex task being performed. Each unit has only very simple patterns of responses to the messages it receives, and generally little or no awareness of other units or the environment outside its immediate vicinity. In some cases, the only communication may be between a unit and its environment.

▶ *Emergence*. A feature of some interactive systems: complex, ordered patterns of behaviour, which are a property of the system as a whole, arise from the simple, interactive behaviour of the system's component parts.

▶ *Adaptation*. The ability of some unit to alter its longer-term behaviour patterns in response to challenges from its environment.

▶ *Selection*. The sifting out of units whose characteristics and behaviour make them less capable of responding successfully to the problems thrown up by their environment. Units that are better fitted for survival will flourish as a result.

Notice that I've used the neutral word 'unit' here. Of course, a unit could be a single creature, such as a member of an ant swarm or a migrating bird. On the other hand, it could also be some internal part of the body of a creature, such as in our insect-walking examples. It could even be something quite abstract, as we'll see in Units 3 and 4.

You may still find all this rather difficult to relate to computing. Although in this unit I introduced a few examples of computer-based systems to illustrate my main points, I agree that the discussion has been rather abstract. However, the four principles discussed in this unit are the backbone of the rest of the course, and they will come up time and time again in future units. In the next two units, I intend to be rather more rigorous: I will try to fill out our line of argument with some theory and illustrate how powerful, practical computer systems yielding valuable results can be built on the back of the principles of interaction, emergence, adaptation and selection.

Now look back at the learning outcomes for this unit and check these against what you think you can now do. Return to any section of the unit if you need to.

Unit 3: Interaction and emergence in swarms

CONTENTS

1	**Introduction to Unit 3**		**72**
	What you need to study this unit		73
	Learning outcomes for Unit 3		74
2	**Interaction and emergence – swarms**		**75**
	2.1	Why study swarms?	75
	2.2	Optimisation problems	75
	2.3	Ant colony optimisation (ACO)	78
	2.4	Particle swarm optimisation (PSO)	101
	2.5	Other applications of swarm concepts	105
3	**Conclusions – swarm intelligence**		**113**
4	**Summary of Unit 3**		**114**
	References and further reading		**167**
	Acknowledgements		**169**
	Index for Block 3		**170**

Introduction to Unit 3

In the previous unit, I isolated four mechanisms which, operating alone or together, may explain how the goal-directed, systematic behaviour of living things – natural intelligence – comes about. They were interaction, emergence, adaptation and selection. I now want to consider how this understanding of the way biological systems work has influenced modern computing and AI. In Unit 1 of this block I introduced the concept of biologically inspired computing or nouvelle AI. Work in this area generally falls into two overlapping categories:

▶ **Scientific investigation**. Building a computer model of a biological system (or any other system found in nature) helps us to understand the properties of natural systems. A computer model enables scientists to:

- make predictions;
- check to what extent the behaviour of the system corresponds with the natural reality;
- vary key parameters of the model and so clarify their influence on the way the system works.

Think back for a moment to the previous unit. This is exactly what you were doing with the ant foraging simulation of Computer Exercise 2.1. Computer modelling is a major weapon in the armoury of the twenty-first-century scientist.

▶ **Software design**. As you will learn in this unit and the next, it is possible to build computer systems, based on the four mechanisms of natural intelligence, that can solve complex practical problems in commerce, design, economics and medicine. This certainly does *not* mean that software engineers building such a system have to stick slavishly to the facts of nature, and build perfectly accurate models of ant colonies, simple animals, and so on. The term 'biologically inspired' reflects this fact: a biologically *inspired* system may be anything from a precise computational model of everything that is known about a natural system, to a system whose design may just reflect a few of the general principles of its natural counterpart.

Although these two activities are different enterprises, both of them involve building a model, based on some aspect of the natural world. In Block 1 I suggested a straightforward definition of the idea of a model as a simplified picture of reality. A computer model, I claimed, is a model in just this sense: a pared-down representation on a computer of some aspect of reality.

More abstractly, a scientific or computer model isolates a few relevant **variables**, the values of which are related to one another according to known **rules**. Some of these variables will be **parameters**: that is, they are *measurable*, and varying them is likely to affect the behaviour of the system. Other variables may be **hidden**: they are not directly observable, but are necessary in order to relate other variables to one another. For example, a computer model of a national economy might have parameters such as gross domestic product, inflation, money in circulation, etc. Hidden variables might be features such as confidence and liquidity. The rules would be known economic laws, such as supply and demand.

Returning to the two main kinds of biologically inspired computing, we will have little to say about the first of these, scientific investigation, in the remainder of this course. I'll mainly be concentrating on the second endeavour – building practical computer systems based on the four mechanisms. For the rest of this unit, I have two main aims:

▶   to delve a little more deeply into the theoretical aspects of our four mechanisms;

▶   to describe and analyse a number of systems built on biological principles, showing how this theory can be put into practice in the design of computer systems capable of solving difficult practical problems.

A quick word of warning and encouragement. The only serious way to analyse the operations of complex systems is to use the language of mathematics. Many of you will be familiar with mathematical notation; others of you will be less so, or may even be intimidated by it. However, in this course we are only using mathematics as a compact and unambiguous way of expressing complex ideas, a powerful shorthand. If you are puzzled by any of the mathematical expressions you meet, please refer to the Maths Guide for the course, where there are full explanations of all the notations and symbols I use.

Exercise 3.1 (optional)

If you lack confidence in your ability to interpret mathematical notation, you may wish to look through the sections of the Maths Guide now.

What you need to study this unit

You will need the following course components, and will need to use your computer and internet connection for some of the exercises.

▶   this Block 3 text

▶   the course DVD.

LEARNING OUTCOMES FOR UNIT 3

After studying this unit you will be able to:

1   write a detailed explanation of the structure of optimisation problems and various ways of representing them;

2   explain, with examples, some of the principles of solving optimisation problems by means of swarms of simple agents;

3   outline the main principles of ant colony optimisation (ACO) and give an example of its practical application;

4   outline the main principles of particle swarm optimisation (PSO);

5   give examples of other applications of swarms of robotic agents.

2 Interaction and emergence – swarms

In this unit, I'm going to discuss two types of computer system built on the principles of interaction and emergence, both of which take their inspiration from the behaviour that arises from interactions among *swarms* of simple agents. The first of these, **ant colony optimisation** (ACO) is based on ideas from biological examples I've already presented, the collective behaviours of colonies of social insects. The second, **particle swarm optimisation** (PSO), draws its inspiration from models of bird flocking and social behaviour in human societies.

2.1 Why study swarms?

Apart from the question of sheer scientific interest, one of the motives I suggested above for research into any form of biologically inspired computing, there are a number of practical reasons for understanding and applying the intelligence of swarms. For the purposes of this unit, I just want to highlight two:

▶ Swarm intelligence may be particularly useful in solving optimisation and data mining problems.

▶ Scientists and engineers are becoming increasingly interested in the idea of **swarm robotics** – large groups of simple robots working collectively, without central direction and control.

I introduced the concept of an optimisation problem in Block 1, and I will expand on the idea in the next subsection. As for swarm robotics, although the field is still in its infancy, it has many potential applications. Tasks which are too arduous, dangerous or inaccessible for human labour are clear contenders. But perhaps the most striking endeavour in which swarm robots have a place is in the branch of **nanotechnology** known as **nanorobotics**. Nanorobots are designed to manipulate objects with nanometre-scale dimensions (a nanometre (nm) is one thousand millionth of a metre, written as 10^{-9} m), so nanorobots interact with objects the size of atoms and molecules and therefore are likely to be of molecular size themselves. It is difficult to see how nanorobot swarms could be controlled by any means other than by the kinds of swarm techniques we will visit in this unit.

An atom has a diameter of roughly 0.1–0.2 nm. A molecule will be greater than 2 nm in size.

Nanotechnology may bring about major scientific and technological breakthroughs, ranging from very fast computers to self-replicating robot swarms, and may be applicable in countless areas of medicine, science and engineering: cellular repair; space exploration robots; DNA readers, manipulators and computers – the promise is endless. Nanotechnology may be one of the defining technologies of the twenty-first century. We will discuss this prospect more fully in Block 6.

2.2 Optimisation problems

Before we start to consider the theory and applications of these two strategies, though, let's first review some of the theoretical background to **optimisation problems** in general.

You may recall that we introduced this class of problems in Block 1. Test your memory and understanding with this question.

SAQ 3.1

What, in general, is an optimisation problem? What is a combinatorial optimisation problem (COP)? Give an example of a COP.

ANSWER..

In general terms, an optimisation problem is simply one in which it is necessary to find the best possible solution from among a number of alternatives. In a combinatorial optimisation problem, the solution will be the best possible *combination* of elements of some given set, such as in the scheduling of jobs in a factory.

Seen in these abstract terms, a huge proportion of the problems we look to computers to solve for us are optimisation problems. And because they are so important, many computational strategies have been developed to tackle them. Without going into any detail, the approaches that have been taken can be roughly divided into the following:

▶ *Exact algorithms.* These try to find the *best* solution and to prove that it is the best.

▶ *Approximate algorithms.* These aim to find *good* solutions within a reasonable length of computing time.

Exact algorithms tend to perform poorly on most real-world problems, so approximate algorithms are almost always needed. These in turn fall into two classes:

▶ *Construction algorithms.* These involve building a possible solution step by step, at each step picking the most plausible candidate from the set of possibilities. Construction algorithms are very quick and can produce good results, but they may completely miss many of the best solutions, so they are often augmented with:

▶ *Local search algorithms.* These start with a plausible solution, maybe generated by a construction algorithm, and then tinker with it, checking if better solutions can be found by making small alterations at various points.

The theory and practice of optimisation algorithms is a huge subject within computing, so I can do no more than present the very brief outline above.

Formally expressed, and simplified slightly, a typical COP consists of the following:

▶ a finite set of *components* $N = \{n_1, n_2, ..., n_i\}$;

▶ a set of *constraints* C;

▶ many *states*, which are ordered sequences of components $\delta = <n_q, n_b, ..., n_j>, <n_s, n_i, ..., n_k> ...$, etc. The set of all possible sequences of components is Δ; and a subset of this set Δ' represents all the *feasible states* allowable under the constraints in C;

▶ a *neighbourhood structure*, defining which states it is possible to move to in one step from a certain state. The *feasible neighbourhood* of a state δ is the set of all states that can be reached from δ in one valid transition, provided that these states are all in Δ';

▶ one or more *solutions* S, that are sets made up of elements of Δ' and which satisfy the problem requirements;

▶ a *cost* associated with each solution S.

To put this into context, recall the Travelling Salesman Problem (TSP) I gave as an example in Block 1, as represented in Table 3.1.

Table 3.1 Specimen TSP

	Exeter	Bristol	Manchester	Leeds	London
Exeter	X	74	236	278	173
Bristol	74	X	165	207	119
Manchester	236	165	X	43	198
Leeds	278	207	43	X	195
London	173	119	198	195	X

To see how well my theoretical description above maps onto this TSP, try the following exercise.

Exercise 3.2

Note down, for each element of the formal description above, what aspect of the TSP corresponds to it.

Discussion ....

I would have answered as follows:

▶ the *components* $N = \{n_1, n_2, ..., n_j\}$ are the cities;

▶ one *constraint* we identified earlier is that each city may be visited once only;

▶ a *state* would be a sequence of cities e.g. {Manchester, Leeds} or {Manchester, Leeds, London, Bristol, Exeter}; a feasible state would be {Manchester, Bristol}, an infeasible one would be {Manchester, Leeds, Manchester};

▶ if there are no constraints on routes between one city and another, the neighbourhood structure shows that it is possible to move from one city to any other. The feasible neighbourhood of the state {Manchester, Leeds} would thus comprise the states {Manchester, Leeds, Bristol}, {Manchester, Leeds, Exeter} and {Manchester, Leeds, London};

▶ a possible *solution* would be the ordered set {Exeter, Bristol, Manchester, Leeds, London};

▶ the *cost* of this solution would be the number of miles it covers.

A convenient way to represent combinatorial optimisation problems formally is to use a branch of mathematics called **graph theory**. A graph-theoretic representation of a COP would be made up as follows. The problem can be visualised as a graph $G = (N, A)$ that is a set of *nodes* $N = \{n_1, n_2, ..., n_i\}$ connected by a set of weighted *edges*. Figure 3.1 illustrates what I mean.

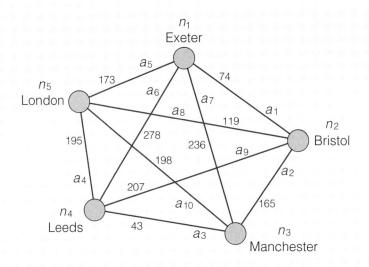

Figure 3.1   TSP graph

Note that I've deliberately drawn this *not* to correspond to anything like the geographical reality. Our graph is a purely abstract expression of the problem space. Relating this to the formal description of COPs above, we can see that:

▶ the components $n_1, ..., n_i$ are nodes on the graph;

▶ the states δ are paths on the graph;

▶ the edges a are valid transitions defining the neighbourhood structure;

▶ the weights on each edge are the cost of making that transition.

You should be clear that the formal and graph-theoretic expressions of a COP are equivalent and can be applied to any COP, not just the TSP.

Much of this may seem familiar from your study of representation and search in Block 2. Many, perhaps most, problems in AI can be seen in abstract terms as optimisation problems. With this background, let's now turn to ant colony optimisation.

2.3   Ant colony optimisation (ACO)

Look back briefly at the description of the experiments carried out by Deneubourg et al. (1990) in Case Study 2.1 in Unit 2 of this block. You may recall that with the set-up depicted in Figure 3.2 the experimenters found that within a very short space of time ants released from the colony towards the food source all congregated on one branch or the other. If the length of one branch was gradually extended, the ants tended to select the shorter of the two paths.

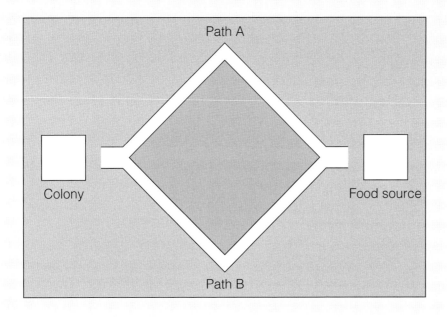

Figure 3.2   Deneubourg's ant foraging experiment (1)

SAQ 3.2

What significant features of this experiment did we single out in the discussion?

ANSWER...

The experiment demonstrated a number of significant characteristics. Firstly, the choice of path was a *collective* decision of the many ants taking part in the process. An individual ant has far too limited a set of behaviours to be able to reason about the best path to take. Secondly, the ants did communicate with one another, but their messages could only be very simple, local and transient. Thirdly, I noted that the choice of path builds up over time as a result of many interactions between the ants.

In Computer Exercise 2.1, you also looked in some detail at a simulation of foraging behaviour, which should have given you a deeper insight into what is going on. Now let's try to consider in a bit more depth why and how the organised behaviour builds up.

Principles of ACO

One quite basic feature of the behaviour modelled in the Computer Exercise 2.1 simulation was that, with no pheromone stimulus, an ant just wanders around at random. In other words, at the most basic level the behaviour of the system is somehow based on *randomness*. The fact of an individual ant, or the whole colony, settling into one path or another is all to do with *probabilities*, rather than the clear-cut, yes/no decisions found in, say, a conventional computer program. We call this sort of behaviour **probabilistic** or **stochastic**. With this in mind, now try the following exercise.

Exercise 3.3

Given that the activities of individual members of the colony are essentially random, how does the colony settle into one path? How should progressively lengthening one of the alternative paths affect the overall behaviour emerging over time?

Discussion ....

Initially, ants will move onto Path A or Path B more or less randomly. Thereafter, the tendency to move to one of these paths gets *reinforced*, while choice of the other is *suppressed*. As time passes, this process builds to a point where one of the paths is abandoned. Lengthening one of the paths initially makes little difference, but eventually it becomes so long that greater pheromone decay ensures that it becomes less attractive to further ants.

Experiments have shown that the probability of the short branch being selected increases in proportion to the ratio r of the lengths of the two branches. When $r \geq 2$ the short branch is almost always selected, although sometimes ants can become locked into the longer path.

There seem to be four main processes at work here:

▶ *Positive feedback*. This is the reinforcement process I referred to in my suggested answer above. As soon as some ants appear on one path, they will lay pheromone trails that encourage other ants to join them. As you learned in Unit 2, this process is termed 'recruitment'. The new ants joining the path will lay more pheromone, which will recruit more ants, and so on, in an amplifying feedback loop.

▶ *Amplification of fluctuations*. One path is favoured over the other simply as a result of some small random fluctuation at the start. Possibly one or two more ants find their way initially onto Path A rather than Path B, and this tiny imbalance gets amplified by positive feedback.

▶ *Negative feedback*. At the same time, the less-frequented path has less and less pheromone deposited on it, and so becomes less and less attractive to other ants. In more complex foraging behaviour, negative feedback may work in other ways as well: food sources become exhausted and abandoned, insufficient numbers of foragers are available, trails become overcrowded, and so on.

▶ *Multiple interactions*. As I've stressed all along, the collective behaviour of the colony emerges from the interactions among its members, and between them and their environment. Your experiments in Computer Exercise 2.2 should have demonstrated that a certain minimum population density is necessary for this emergent behaviour to arise. The interactions may be either *direct*, through pheromone trails, for instance, or *stigmergic*. Look back at the previous unit if you have forgotten the precise meaning of this term.

Many theorists argue that the randomness at the root of the colony's emergent behaviour is vitally necessary for its healthy functioning. As we've noted, random fluctuations are amplified into organised behaviour. But simple positive feedback on its own can lead to stagnation, exhaustion and vulnerability. Random fluctuations also make it possible for the colony to break out of unprofitable reinforced behaviour, discover new food sources and form useful novel patterns.

Ant colonies are therefore self-organised systems whose behaviour is an emergent property of probabilistic internal interactions.

SAQ 3.3

Quickly recall and note down some of the main features of emergent behaviour.

ANSWER...

Emergent patterns have some of the following characteristics: they occur in an initially homogenous medium; they are structures persisting in space and time in that medium, like gliders; they may have multiple stable states at the same time; they can exhibit bifurcations, i.e. sudden changes of behaviour.

We've already noted that the ants walk randomly in the absence of pheromone stimulation. However, that is not necessarily the end of probabilistic behaviour. In most models, the presence of pheromone does not absolutely determine that an ant will move towards it. It *biases* the ant's behaviour towards one choice or another, rather than definitely deciding for it. The presence of pheromone on a trail only makes it more probable that it will follow that path, with an increase in probability that is proportional to the amount of pheromone present. This is illustrated in the model evolved by Deneubourg et al. (1990), which was shown to agree very well with the behaviour observed in his experiments with real ants.

Here is the model. Starting with the assumption that the amount of pheromone deposited on a path is proportional to the number of ants that have used it, and that there is no pheromone decay over time, let A_i and B_i be the number of ants that have moved onto branches A and B after i ants have travelled from the colony to the source. The pheromone concentration on each branch is τ_{ia} and τ_{ib} respectively, and the probability P_A that the $i + 1$th ant will choose branch A, is given by:

$$P_A = \frac{(k + \tau_{ia})^\alpha}{(k + \tau_{ia})^\alpha + (k + \tau_{ib})^\alpha} \tag{3.1}$$

where k and α are constants. Since alternative probabilities must always add up to 1, the probability P_B that the $i + 1$th ant will choose branch B is:

$$P_B = (1 - P_A) \tag{3.2}$$

You can see from Equation 3.1 that the probability of choosing branch A is simply the amount of pheromone on A divided by the sum of the concentrations on branch A and branch B, modulated by two parameters k and α that can be varied from experiment to experiment. The parameter α determines how powerful an attractant small differences in pheromone concentration are: when α is high, a slightly higher concentration on one branch over another will mean a very high probability of an ant choosing that branch; when it is low, it will still bias an ant's choice, but much less strongly. Parameter k is a measure of how attractive a poorly marked path will be: if k is low, paths with greater amounts of pheromone tend to be chosen; as k grows higher, the probability of a poorly-marked path being chosen increases, the probability coming closer and closer to - although never reaching - 0.5 (purely random), with increasing k.

Exercise 3.4

An ant faced with the choice between paths A or B senses 19.2 units of pheromone on branch A and only 3.6 on B. If α is 1.8 and k is 17.9, what are the respective probabilities of the ant choosing branch A and branch B? How will changing α to 0.9 and k to 25.4 affect the relative probabilities P_A and P_B?

Discussion ....

All we need to do is plug these values into Equation 3.1. We get:

$$P_A = \frac{(17.9 + 19.2)^{1.8}}{(17.9 + 19.2)^{1.8} + (17.9 + 3.6)^{1.8}}$$

$$= \frac{37.1^{1.8}}{37.1^{1.8} + 21.5^{1.8}}$$

$$= \frac{668.15}{668.15 + 250.26}$$

$$= \frac{668.15}{918.41}$$

$$= 0.73$$

Then from Equation 3.2, we can easily see that $P_B = 1 - 0.73 = 0.27$.

Changing the values of α and k:

$$P_A = \frac{(25.4 + 19.2)^{0.9}}{(25.4 + 19.2)^{0.9} + (25.4 + 3.6)^{0.9}}$$

$$= \frac{44.6^{0.9}}{44.6^{0.9} + 29.0^{0.9}}$$

$$= \frac{30.51}{30.51 + 20.71}$$

$$= \frac{30.51}{51.22}$$

$$= 0.60$$

P_B is thus 0.40. You can see that the higher value of k in this case has made the poorly marked branch B rather more attractive.

Equations 3.1 and 3.2 tell us the probability of an ant taking a particular path. In Deneubourg et al.'s model, the actual choice is made as follows: the $i + 1$th ant will choose path A or B according to the following rule:

A if $\delta \le P_A$

B if $\delta > P_A$ (3.3)

The generalisation of this equation to more than one choice is covered in later examples.

where δ is a random variable between 0 and 1. You can see from the formulae in Equation 3.3 how randomness and probability are intimately related in this kind of stochastic system. Deneubourg found that $\alpha \approx 2$ and $k \approx 20$ gave an almost perfect fit with his observations of real ant behaviour in the two-path experiment.

SAQ 3.4

Look back quickly at Deneubourg's later experiment, illustrated in Figure 2.3 of Unit 2. What did the results of this suggest about the path decisions that real ants seem to make?

ANSWER...

They suggested that ants may also be biased towards choosing paths by factors other than local pheromone concentrations. They may make decisions based on individual memories of the terrain they are traversing.

In choosing a trail, ants may not simply be reacting to an immediate pheromone stimulus. Individual foragers may retain memories of paths travelled already and these memories can contribute to their choice of path. This consideration will be important, as we now come to discuss artificial ant colonies.

Artificial ants for optimisation

In your study of ant behaviour in the experiments of Deneubourg et al., and in your own observations of the simulated foraging of Computer Exercise 2.1, you may have noted that the ants are doing something rather like the kinds of search we've encountered in our discussion of optimisation problems. Without central control or planning, they are finding efficient paths from a source to a goal, sometimes via intermediate points. Indeed, certain species of ants build immense networks of nests, connected by more or less permanent pheromone trails, laid along highly cost-effective networks of paths. In other words, by finding the shortest and most efficient paths through a network of trails, the insects are collectively solving optimisation problems. How can we take this insight and use it in practical optimisation systems?

There have been a number of specific approaches to this task in the past decade, some of which I'll examine in a moment, but they all have features in common:

▶ The problem is represented as a weighted graph, in the manner I suggested in the section on optimisation problems above.

▶ n virtual ants (think of the NetLogo turtles set-up in Computer Exercise 2.1) are released to move, concurrently and asynchronously, across this graph, from node to node.

▶ From its present position, each ant chooses the next node on the graph to move to according to a **transition rule**, based on information available at its current node.

▶ As they move across the graph, ants build up solutions step by step; a complete solution (in the case of the TSP, every city visited once) I will from now on call a **tour**.

▶ Ants may release (virtual) pheromone as they cross each edge; alternatively, they may complete a tour and then deposit pheromone along its whole length, the amount they lay down being a function of how good a solution to the problem the path is. This acts as an agent for recruitment and reinforcement, just as in real ant colonies.

▶ Generally, pheromone evaporates at a certain rate over time, as in Computer Exercise 2.1.

▶ There may also be additional global actions, known as **demon actions**, such as releasing additional pheromone onto some of the best solutions.

You should note that the demon actions have no real counterpart in nature. However, remember my comment at the start of this unit – it is no part of the task of engineers to stick dogmatically to the facts of nature: their task is to find the best, and most imaginative, solutions to the problems in hand.

Exercise 3.5

Based on the features described above, can you sketch out a very general algorithm for optimisation using virtual ants? There is no need to go into great detail; just note down the most basic steps that have to be taken. And don't worry about the representation of the problem as a graph – assume that that has been done already.

Discussion ....

I'll try to fill in most of the details in the next section. However, it would appear that the key steps are:

1 generate the ants and place them at their start states;

2 move the ants step by step, in parallel, towards the goal state, with ants making transitions to a new node at each step, based on the agreed transition rule; finish when the goal state is reached;

3 lay down pheromones;

4 evaporate the pheromones by the specified amount at the end of all the ants' tours;

5 carry out any demon activities;

6 evaluate the results;

7 go back to 1. Stop after a certain number of repetitions.

Now we can use this basic structure to define what is known as the **ant colony metaheuristic** in the next section.

ACO metaheuristic

On the basis of the points above we can draw up a very general algorithm, known as a metaheuristic, for an ant colony approach to optimisation problems. Using a NetLogo-like pseudo-code to represent it, the metaheuristic will look like this:

```
to setup                          ;; repeat until termination condition
    setup_graph
    cct N [initialise_ant]        ;; creates and initialises N ants
end


to go
    ask turtles [move_ant]        ;; move every ant
    ask graph [evaporate_pheromone] ;; evaporate pheromone from edges
    demon_actions                 ;; any optional actions
end
```

Although it's very general, this should be clear enough. The setup_graph procedure may involve laying down a small amount of pheromone on every edge of the graph, to start the process off. All ant activity is then carried out in parallel until some termination condition (pressing a STOP button, say).

Looking back at the general features of artificial ant algorithms in the previous section, note that there may be either a policy of depositing pheromone on a transition edge as soon as the ant moves along that edge to a new node (step-by-step update), or one of releasing pheromone only along a fully completed trail (delayed update). These alternatives appear in the fuller specification of the procedure move_ant:

```
to move_ant
    ifelse not(current_node = target_node)
    [    set Prob compute_transition_probabilities [[Memory, Ω]
            ;; Ω is the set of problem constraints
        ant_transition_rule [Prob, Ω]
        move_to_next_node
        if [step_by_step_update]
        [    release_pheromone_on_edge_traversed
            set Memory update_memory ;; updates its memory
        ]
    ]
    [    if [delayed_update]
            release_pheromone_on_edges_visited [Memory]
    ]
end
```

The ant memory usually just contains the path that that ant has traversed up to its current point. The situation of a virtual ant situated at node i is summed up in Figure 3.3. (η_{ij} is a special term which I'll introduce shortly.)

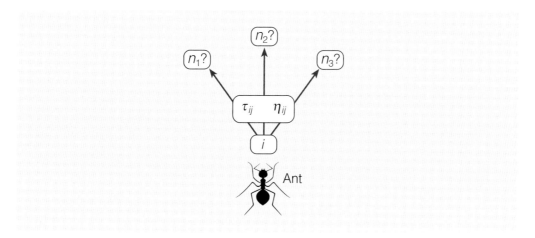

Figure 3.3   Ant decision point at node i

Remember, this is only pseudo-code, giving the shape of the algorithm. The description is still very general; but most – though not absolutely all – artificial ant-colony systems used for optimisation are variations on this basic pattern. The key features of any specific algorithm will be the two procedures `compute_transition_probabilities()` and `ant_transition_rule()`. The exact specification of the `evaporate_pheromone()` and `demon_actions()` procedures are obviously important too. It is here that the main points of difference between the various ant colony systems produced in the last few years lie. Let's now discuss a few of these.

ACO systems and models

To design a practical system for solving optimisation problems using ACO, the engineer has the ACO metaheuristic to build upon. However, this is no more than a basic framework: to build a working algorithm, the software engineer will need to give precise meanings to a number of the concepts in it and to make a set of key decisions. For example, given that a graph-theoretic specification of the optimisation problem can be constructed, she will have to decide on:

▶ the exact meaning of the pheromone trails along the edges of the graph; that is, the precise effect they will have on each virtual ant's choice of path. From now on I will refer to this term, the amount of pheromone on an edge joining nodes i and j, as τ_{ij}. In fact, throughout this discussion, the subscripts ij refer to the edge between nodes i and j;

▶ a precise definition of any other information, over and above pheromone stimulus, that might influence an ant sitting at node i to move to node j next. I will refer to this term, called the **heuristic term**, as η_{ij};

▶ how exactly τ_{ij} and η_{ij} are combined to calculate the probability that an ant at node i will choose node j;

▶ what strategies will be used for pheromone update and pheromone evaporation;

▶ which, if any, demon actions will be carried out.

Remember that it is not necessarily the task of the designer to imitate nature. However, a good example of the heuristic term, found in real colonies, would be the tendency I pointed to in Unit 2 for ants to backtrack along a paths as soon as they detect they are moving at right angles to an earlier, more direct, path towards the food source.

SAQ 3.5

Now look back quickly at our earlier section on optimisation problems. What were the two general types of approximate algorithms used to approach them?

ANSWER...

The two main classes of optimisation strategy were *construction* and *local search*.

These two approaches are often combined: a candidate solution is constructed and is then progressively improved by searching locally from each point on the solution path for better choices, a process known as *iterative improvement*. Many ant colony models incorporate local search, including it among the demon actions provided for by the ACO metaheuristic.

Ant System

The first working ACO algorithm, Ant System, was introduced by Dorigo et al. in 1991. In the previous section, I referred to the key decisions needed to turn the metaheuristic into a working reality. The researchers made the following straightforward choices:

▶ *Pheromone trails* τ_{ij}. Pheromone is deposited by every ant at the end of its tour (delayed pheromone update) in an amount proportional to the quality of the tour (i.e. how short a distance it represents).

▶ *Heuristic information* η_{ij}. The relative desirability of the next node j from a position at node i is given by $1 / d_{ij}$, where d_{ij} is simply the distance from node i to node j.

▶ *Probabilistic decision making*. Each ant calculates the probability of moving from its current position at node i to node j by applying the following rule:

$$P_{ij} = \frac{[\tau_{ij}]^{\alpha} \cdot [\eta_{ij}]^{\beta}}{\sum\limits_{k \in N_i} [\tau_{ik}]^{\alpha} \cdot [\eta_{ik}]^{\beta}} \qquad \text{if } j \in N_i \tag{3.4}$$

where N_i is the feasible neighbourhood of node i. If j is not in the feasible neighbourhood of i (i.e. $j \notin N_i$), then the P_{ij} is 0. The two parameters α and β bias the ant's choice either towards the pheromone strength or towards the distance heuristic. If α is 0, then the ant will base its choice entirely on the distance of neighbouring nodes η_{ij}. Conversely, if β is 0, the ant will only use the pheromone strength τ_{ij} as a guide. A very low value of α often leads to poor solutions, while a low value of β can end in stagnation, with the colony locked into an unsatisfactory choice of path.

▶ *Pheromone evaporation and update.* When ants have completed their tours, the pheromone on every edge τ_{ij} is first of all evaporated by a constant factor, given by:

$$\tau_{ij} \leftarrow (1-\rho)\cdot\tau_{ij} \tag{3.5}$$

where ρ is a constant between 0 and 1. Then each ant retraces its steps, using its memory M of nodes it has visited, and releases a certain amount of pheromone on each edge as it passes. The quantity to be deposited, Δ_{ij}, is proportional to the quality of that tour. This is summed up by:

$$\tau_{ij} \leftarrow \tau_{ij} + \Delta_{ij} \qquad \text{for all } ij \text{ in the ant's tour} \tag{3.6}$$

The precise way in which Δ_{ij} is determined depends on the equation:

$$\Delta_{ij} = Q/L \qquad \text{for all } ij \text{ in the ant's tour} \tag{3.7}$$

where L is the length of the tour and Q is a parameter.

▶ *Demon actions.* In the early versions of Ant System, there were no demon actions.

Pulling this all together, and skipping a few of the details, the `move_ant` procedure of the Ant Colony algorithm looks like this:

```
to move_ant
    ifelse not(current_node = target_node)
    [    set Prob compute_transition_probabilities [Memory, Ω]
                ;; for every k in N_current_node, apply Equation 3.4
         ant_transition_rule [Prob, Ω]    ;; apply Equation 3.3
         move_to_next_node
         set Memory update_memory              ;; add new state to M
    ]
    [release_pheromone_on_edges_visited [Memory]]
            ;; apply Equation 3.6
    end
```

Note that the pheromone will have been evaporated from all edges by a global procedure before ants update their own trails. The same procedure also seeds every edge of the graph with a very small initial quantity τ_0 of pheromone to start the whole process going. Ants are distributed to random nodes on the graph during this initialisation procedure. `move_ant` is repeated a number of times n, up to some value n_{max}, after which the algorithm terminates.

Exercise 3.6

A virtual ant is situated at the node Manchester in a (rather simplified) travelling salesman optimisation, using the Ant System algorithm. Its position and feasible neighbourhood is illustrated in Figure 3.4.

If $\alpha = 0.6$ and $\beta = 0.2$, what are the probabilities of the ant visiting Exeter, Bristol and Leeds?

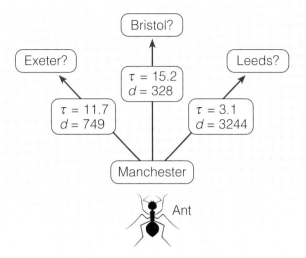

Figure 3.4   Ant decision point in the TSP

Discussion ....

This is just a question of applying some specific values to Equation 3.4. First, convert the distances d_{ij} between cities to the measure η_{ij} for each city ($\eta_{ij} = 1 / d_{ij}$) to get:

$\eta_{\text{Manchester–Exeter}} = 0.0013$,

$\eta_{\text{Manchester–Bristol}} = 0.0030$ and

$\eta_{\text{Manchester–Leeds}} = 0.0003$.

Using Equation 3.4 we can calculate the probabilities as follows:

$$P_{\text{Exeter}} = \left(11.7^{0.6} * 0.0013^{0.2}\right) / \left(\left(11.7^{0.6} * 0.0013^{0.2}\right) + \left(15.2^{0.6} * 0.0030^{0.2}\right) + \left(3.1^{0.6} * 0.0003^{0.2}\right)\right)$$
$$= 1.16 / (1.16 + 1.60 + 0.39)$$
$$= 1.16 / 3.15$$
$$= 0.37$$

$$P_{\text{Bristol}} = \left(15.2^{0.6} * 0.0030^{0.2}\right) / \left(\left(11.7^{0.6} * 0.0013^{0.2}\right) + \left(15.2^{0.6} * 0.0030^{0.2}\right) + \left(3.1^{0.6} * 0.0003^{0.2}\right)\right)$$
$$= 1.60 / (1.16 + 1.60 + 0.39)$$
$$= 1.6 / 3.15$$
$$= 0.51$$

$$P_{\text{Leeds}} = \left(3.1^{0.6} * 0.0003^{0.2}\right) / \left(\left(11.7^{0.6} * 0.0013^{0.2}\right) + \left(15.2^{0.6} * 0.0030^{0.2}\right) + \left(3.1^{0.6} * 0.0003^{0.2}\right)\right)$$
$$= 0.39 / (1.16 + 1.60 + 0.39)$$
$$= 0.39 / 3.15$$
$$= 0.12$$

Dorigo et al. tested Ant System on the TSP, in competition with other well-known general-purpose optimisation algorithms. The results were encouraging: the system worked well on relatively small problems (30–70 cities), and was able to produce, and even improve on, the solutions generated by other general-purpose optimisation systems. Table 3.2, based on results published by Dorigo et al. (1991), summarises these comparisons (the tour length is expressed in whole numbers of kilometres).

Table 3.2 Comparison of optimisation results

System	Best tour length	Average tour length	Standard deviation
Ant System	420	420.4	1.3
Tabu Search	420	420.6	1.5
Simulated Annealing	422	459.8	25.1

However, the results were more disappointing on larger problems (>70 cities). Ant System failed to find the best known solutions to these, although it did fairly rapidly find good solutions. The reason for this is that the best algorithms combine construction with local search. As you will see, later variations on the ACO metaheuristic took this line.

SAQ 3.6

Write a short bulleted list of what you recall as the main principles of Ant System. There is no need to refer back to the details of the equations – just list the main ideas.

ANSWER...

I came up with the following points:

▶ An initialisation procedure seeds every edge of the graph with a small amount of pheromone τ_0, and then distributes a number of ants to nodes on the graph randomly.

▶ Ants make their decision as to which node j to visit from node i by a combination of pheromone stimulus τ_{ij} and heuristic information η_{ij}, based on the reciprocal of the distance from i to j.

▶ Ants combine τ_{ij} and η_{ij} in an equation which yields the relative probabilities of their moving to alternative cities in the feasible neighbourhood of i; using this, they move from node to node, consulting their memory to avoid moving to a node they have visited, until they have completed a full tour.

▶ Pheromone is evaporated globally at the start of each iteration.

▶ After completing a tour, each ant retraces its steps, depositing an amount of pheromone on every edge it has traversed. This amount is proportional to how good a solution its tour represents.

▶ The process is terminated after a certain maximum number of iterations.

We will now look rather more briefly at some later variations on the ACO metaheuristic and then move on to discuss a case study.

Ant Colony System

Ant Colony System (ACS) was one the earliest successors to Ant System, and was proposed by Dorigo and Gambardella (1997). Although quite similar to Ant System in outline, ACS incorporated a number of major modifications to the earlier system:

1   *A new transition rule.* If q_0 is a parameter with a value between 0 and 1 and q is a random variable, an ant at node i selects node j as its next destination according to the following rule:

$$\text{if } q \le q_0$$
$$j = \arg\max_{u \in N_i}\left\{\tau_{iu} \cdot [\eta_{iu}]^{\beta}\right\}$$
$$\text{if } q > q_0 \tag{3.8}$$

$$p_{ij} = \frac{[\tau_{ij}] \cdot [\eta_{ij}]^{\beta}}{\displaystyle\sum_{k \in N_i}[\tau_{ik}] \cdot [\eta_{ik}]^{\beta}} \qquad \text{if } j \in N_i$$

It takes a bit of time to pick one's way through this rule, but in the end you'll find it is quite logical. On certain occasions – decided randomly, when the stochastically varying quantity q is less than or equal to q_0 – the ant will simply pick the best trail, based on the pheromone and heuristic information, with a probability of 1 (i.e. complete certainty). This is the first part of the rule. On all other occasions, it will pick a city from the feasible neighbourhood of i using a probabilistic rule similar to the one in the Ant System. This gives the system a certain amount of freedom to explore new, less promising trails, while often just settling for the best trails known at the time. Just how often depends on the value decided on for q_0 – if it is close to 1, the ants will usually set off for the most plausible destinations; if it is close to 0 they may follow trails that are less well marked by pheromones and heuristic clues.

2   *Global pheromone update.* This is done only after all the ants have completed their tours (i.e. a delayed update strategy) by a demon action. Only the single ant that accomplished the best tour of all is selected for the privilege of doing this update. First of all, pheromone is evaporated from that ant's trail *only*, according to the rule in Equation 3.5. Then an amount of pheromone is deposited on the successful ant's current tour, using Equation 3.6. This time, however, the amount of pheromone to be deposited is given by:

$$\Delta_{ij} = 1/L \tag{3.9}$$

In some versions of ACS this is multiplied by a constant ρ.

3   *Local pheromone update.* This is done as the ants move from edge to edge. Every time it traverses an edge, the ant deposits some pheromone according to the rule:

$$\tau_{ij} \leftarrow (1-\varphi) \cdot \tau_{ij} + \varphi \cdot \tau_0 \tag{3.10}$$

where τ_0 is the amount of pheromone deposited on every trail by the initialisation procedure at the start of the process, and φ is a constant between 0 and 1. Note this constant is only used for local pheromone deposit. For the global release, the constant ρ (which may have a quite different value) is used.

ACS also incorporated a local search procedure. Otherwise, ACS is firmly based on the principles of Ant System. To underline this, try the following exercise.

Exercise 3.7

Sketch out how the ACO metaheuristic would be modified to provide a detailed algorithm for ACS.

Discussion ....

I worked out something like the following, using the NetLogo-like pseudo-code I am using to specify algorithms. S is the set of tours produced by the ants on this iteration.

```
to move_ant
    if not(current_node = target_node)
    [    set Randq random 1
             ;; generate random number between 0 & 1
         set Prob compute_transition_probabilities [Memory, Ω, Randq]
             ;; for every k in N_current_node, apply Equation 3.8
         ant_transition_rule [Prob, Ω]      ;;apply Equations 3.3
```

```
            move_to_next_node
            update_pheromone_trail              ;; apply Equation 3.10
            set Memory update_memory            ;; add new state to M
      ]
      [   evaporate_pheromone_best
                ;; diminish pheromone on best ant's trail only using
                ;; Equation 3.5
            release_pheromone_on_best_edges
                ;; add pheromone on best ant's trail only using
                ;; Equation 3.6 and 3.9
      ]
end
```

```
to demon_actions
      foreach tours                 ;;tours is a list of all the ants' tours
      [
          do_local_search [tour];; find better solutions local to each tour
      ]
      set S_{current_best} = best_solution(S)
      if (better [S_{current_best}, S_{global_best}])
          [set S_{global_best} = S_{current_best}]
      foreach edges_in_tour_S_{global_best}
          [evaporate_pheromone_on_edge]     ;; Apply Equation 3.5
      foreach number_of_edges_in_tour_S_{global_best})
          [deposit_pheromone_on_edge]       ;; Apply Equation 3.6 and 3.9
end
```

Don't worry if you didn't go into as much detail as this. It's important just to get the general idea of how the metaheuristic can be adapted.

Dorigo and Gambardella (1997) announced results that were extremely promising, comparable with the performance of some of the best general-purpose optimisation systems. To illustrate this, Table 3.3 shows comparative results for problems of various sizes. The result in each case is the shortest length of tour produced by the algorithm in whole numbers of kilometres. The ACS algorithm had been supplemented with a local search procedure called 3-opt among its demon actions.

Table 3.3 TSP optimisation results for various algorithms

System	50 cities	75 cities	100 cities
ACS	425	535	21 282
GA	428	545	21 761
EP	426	542	n/a
SA	443	580	n/a

Key: GA = Genetic algorithm – see Block 5; EP = Evolutionary Programming; SA = Simulated Annealing

Other variations on the ACO metaheuristic

There have been numerous improvements and additions to the ACO metaheuristic since Dorigo et al.'s (1991) work. To describe these in any detail would take up too much valuable space, so here is the briefest summary of some of them.

▶ Max–Min Ant System (Stützle and Hoos, 1996). The permissible strength of a pheromone trail is limited to a value between τ_{min} and τ_{max}. Pheromone trails are initialised at the start to a value close to τ_{max}.

▶ Rank-Based Ant System (Bullenheimer et al., 1997). On each iteration, after ants have completed their tours they are ranked according to quality. The n best ants are allowed to deposit a quantity of pheromone proportional to its rank and the quality of its solution. A demon deposits an additional amount of pheromone on the path followed by the globally best ant.

▶ Best–Worst Ant System (Cordon et al., 2002). Greater quantities of pheromone are evaporated from the trail of the worst ant on each iteration, penalising poor solutions. Additionally, an idea is borrowed from evolutionary computing (see Block 5): a demon occasionally *mutates* the amount of pheromone on the edges leading to and from a selected node, by a certain amount. The node, the amount and when to carry out the mutation are all decided probabilistically.

All these system use the same, or very similar, transition rules to Ant System. The developers of all the above systems have announced very good results.

SAQ 3.7

What do you think the researchers were trying to achieve in each of the modifications to Ant System described above?

ANSWER..

In each case the amendments seem designed to reinforce the trails of ants that have performed well, but at the same time to encourage ants to explore new paths.

All combinatorial optimisation algorithms face this same basic problem. There has to be a trade-off between reinforcing and improving the good solutions that have been generated, and the need to look for radically new solutions that might not be so promising at first but could be improved to become much better than the existing ones. Reinforcing good solutions can lead to *stagnation*, with the system becoming stuck with sets of results that are OK, but poorer than the best possible. But striking out in drastically new directions (*innovation*) can lead nowhere and may slow down the algorithm to the point of its becoming useless. Look back at the three models you've studied above: you can see that in every case the modifications are all designed to address this problem.

Computer Exercise 3.1

Complete Computer Exercise 3.1 on the course DVD.

Real ants versus artificial ants

All this may seem quite far from nature, remote from the behaviour of the real ants you encountered in the previous unit. Before we move on to consider a case study of ACO, let's try to sum up the differences and the similarities between the artificial ants of Ant System, ACS and the others, and the living, crawling ants of Unit 2.

Exercise 3.8

Sum up briefly what you think are the main similarities and differences between real and artificial ants?

Discussion ....

You might have noted some of the following points: both real and artificial ants collaborate to generate emergent solutions to optimisation problems. In both cases the collaboration is through pheromone communication; and both kinds of ant base their choice of path on stochastic transition procedures.

However, as well as pheromone information, artificial ants make use of heuristic information, such as the distance measures in the TSP, which is generally not available to the real insects. Moreover, artificial ants retain memories of paths they have travelled; and since the amount of pheromone they deposit is often dependent on the quality of the solution they have generated, then artificial ants are also making use of global information that a real ant would not be aware of. There can be no demon actions such as local search optimisation in real ant colonies.

Summing this up, the key similarities between real and artificial ants are:

▶ collective action to construct optimal solutions;

▶ stigmergic communication, based on pheromones;

▶ pheromone evaporation;

▶ stochastic decision making.

The main differences are:

▶ use of heuristic information;

▶ ant memories;

▶ use of global information;

▶ pheromone evaporation – although pheromones do decay, they are generally much longer lived in nature than they are presumed to be in artificial ant systems. Indeed, the undeniable fact that real pheromones may persist for quite a long time is still an obstacle to understanding how biological ant systems function;

▶ demon actions – these have no real counterparts in nature.

These differences may irk some purists, who insist that biologically inspired computing should stick to the facts of nature, but the best ant colony simulations have produced excellent solutions to difficult real-life problems, as illustrated in the following case study.

Case Study 3.1: Optimisation of telecommunications routing

Telecommunications networks are systems of physical connectors – cables, microwave connections, fibre optics, satellite links – linking together a set of points (nodes) where messages can be sent and received. In an ideal world, a network would be fully connected, as in Figure 3.5, with a direct connection between every node and every other node.

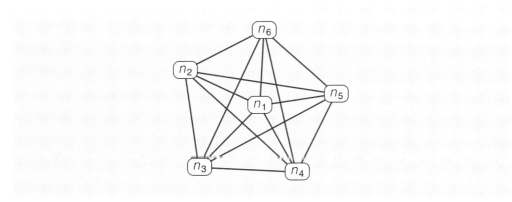

Figure 3.5   A fully connected network

However, for anything other than the smallest local net, this would be utterly impractical; the cost would be prohibitive. In real networks, then, a call or message is passed from its source node *s* to destination *d* via a series of intermediate points, or **switches** (see Figure 3.6). As soon as a call is initiated, a procedure must be activated to decide on the most suitable path for the message to take through the web of switches, a procedure known as **routing**.

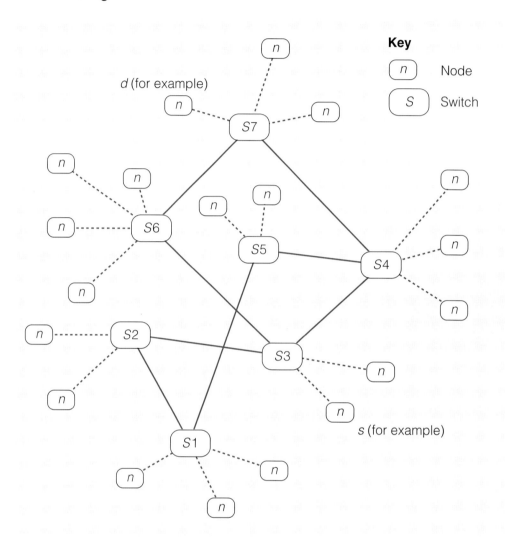

Figure 3.6   Switched network

You can see already that this looks like a classic problem in combinatorial optimisation. So it is, but there is rather more to it than that. The problems we considered earlier were *static* ones. For example, in the TSP the towns, the routes between them and the associated distances don't change. However, network routing is a *dynamic* problem. It is dynamic in *space*, because the shape of the network – its **topology** – may change: switches and nodes may break down and new ones may come on line. But the problem is also dynamic in *time*, and quite unpredictably so. The amount of network traffic will vary constantly: some switches may become overloaded, there may be local bursts of activity that make parts of the network very slow, and so on. So network routing is a very difficult problem of dynamic optimisation. Finding fast, effcient and intelligent routing algorithms is a major headache for telcommunications engineers and computer scientists.

In 1996 a group of scientists led by Ruud Schoonderwoerd developed a prototype system, called ABC, for network routing based on ant colony optimisation. Clearly the routing problem can be represented as a graph, as a communications network is itself a graph. Consider the miniature network represented in Figure 3.7. In the ABC model, each node has a capacity C, a spare capacity S and a routing table. The routing table of node N_5 in Figure 3.7 is shown in Table 3.4. The table has $n = 3$ rows, corresponding to the n nodes that are the nearest neighbours of N_5. Each of the $d = 4$ columns represents possible final destination nodes for a call or an ant arriving at N_5. The values in the table cells r_{nd} are used by both calls and ants to select the next node to move to.

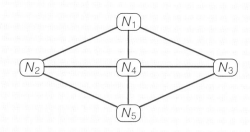

Figure 3.7   Sample network

Table 3.4 Routing table of node N_5

Destination	N_1	N_2	N_3	N_4
Neighbour				
N_2	0.60	0.50	0.10	0.10
N_3	0.30	0.20	0.70	0.30
N_4	0.10	0.30	0.20	0.60

SAQ 3.8

What is the probability that an arrival at node N_5 destined for node N_2 will move to node N_3?

ANSWER..
Very easy. It can just be read off from the table as 0.20.

Calls themselves move around the network completely deterministically. A call arriving at node i simply consults the routing table and takes the path to the neighbour node with the highest value: there is no element of probability. So a call bound for node N_1 arriving at N_5 will select node N_2 as its next step, since its value, at 0.6, is the highest available for that destination. For calls, then, the values in the routing table represent not probabilities, but the relative *desirability* of moving to other nodes.

However, virtual ants also move around the network, their task being to constantly adjust the routing tables according to the latest information about network conditions. For an ant, the values in the table are *probabilities* that their next move will be to a certain node. The progress of an ant around the network is governed by the following informal rules:

▶ Ants start at random nodes.

▶ They move around the network from node to node, using the routing table at each node as a guide to which link to cross next.

▶ As it explores, an ant *ages*, the age of each individual being related to the length of time elapsed since it set out from its source. However, an ant that finds itself at a congested node is delayed, and thus made to age faster than ants moving through less choked areas. Various schemes can be used to calculate this delay: Schoonderwoerd et al. (1996) used the formula:

$$D = c \cdot e^{-d \cdot S} \qquad (3.11)$$

where S is the spare capacity of the node, and c and d are parameters (e is the mathematical constant). This was found to give good results.

▶ As an ant crosses a link between two nodes, it deposits pheromone. In the ABC model, however, it leaves it not on the edge itself, but on the entry for that edge in the routing table of each node it is leaving. An ant at node i which has just arrived from node j and which started its journey at node s will leave pheromone on i's routing table entry r_{js}, by reinforcing the value it finds there. Other values in that column of i's table are decreased, in a process analogous to pheromone decay.

▶ When ant reaches its final destination it is presumed to have died and is deleted from the system.

To illustrate this, consider the situation of the ant in Figure 3.8. It has just arrived at node N_5 from N_3, having started at node N_4. Therefore, the entry r_{34} in N_5's routing table r will be increased, while the other k entries in column 4 of r, r_{k4}, are decreased. All other values are unchanged.

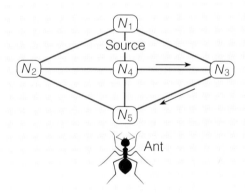

Figure 3.8   Ant decision point at node N_5

The new value $r_{js}(t+1)$ of the entry $r_{js}(t)$ that the ant reinforces is given by the formula:

$$r_{js}(t+1) = \frac{r_{js}(t) + \delta r}{1 + \delta r} \qquad (3.12)$$

The decay of the other values in the target column is calculated by:

$$r_{ks}(t+1) = \frac{r_{ks}(t)}{1 + \delta r} \qquad (3.13)$$

The value δr is a parameter determined by the age of the ant in question. Schoonderwoerd et al. calculated δr by means of the formula:

$$\delta r = \frac{a}{T} + b \qquad (3.14)$$

where T is the length of time the ant has spent in the network and a and b are parameters. Fixing the values of these parameters as $a = 0.05$, $b = 0.06$, try the following exercise.

Exercise 3.9

Having started at node N_4, an ant arrives at N_5 via N_3, in the network depicted in Figure 3.8 above. Assuming it has been in the network for 15.4 time units, what effect will it have on the routing table of N_5 (shown above in Table 3.4)?

Discussion ....

First of all, we must work out the value of δr for this ant. Applying Equation 3.14 we get $\delta r = 0.05 / 15.4 + 0.06 = 0.063$. Now we can use this value in Equations 3.12 and 3.13 to calculate the changes to N_5's routing table. Since the ant's ultimate source s is N_4, only the rightmost of the four columns will be affected. The ant has just come from N_3, so the value $r_{34}(t)$ is reinforced using Equation 3.12 as follows:

$$
\begin{aligned}
r_{34}(t + 1) &= (r_{34}(t) + 0.063) / (1 + 0.063) \\
&= (0.3 + 0.063) / (1 + 0.063) \\
&= 0.363 / 1.063 \\
&= 0.341.
\end{aligned}
$$

The other two values in that column are diminished by pheromone evaporation using Equation 3.13 as follows:

$$
\begin{aligned}
r_{24}(t)(t + 1) &= r_{24}(t) / (1 + 0.063) \\
&= 0.1 / (1 + 0.063) \\
&= 0.1 / 1.063 \\
&= 0.094
\end{aligned}
$$

$$
\begin{aligned}
r_{44}(t + 1) &= r_{44}(t) / (1 + 0.063) \\
&= 0.6 / (1 + 0.063) \\
&= 0.6 / 1.063 \\
&= 0.564
\end{aligned}
$$

With a little bit of rounding, the new routing table for N_5 is as shown in Table 3.5.

Table 3.5 Updated routing table for node N_5

Destination / Neighbour	N_1	N_2	N_3	N_4
N_2	0.60	0.50	0.10	**0.09**
N_3	0.30	0.20	0.70	**0.34**
N_4	0.10	0.30	0.20	**0.56**

Remember that the values in each column are probabilities, so applying Equations 3.12 and 3.13 together must (and does) preserve the property that these probabilities sum to 1 (allowing for rounding).

SAQ 3.9

What will be the overall effect of making the parameter δr depend on the age of the ant?

ANSWER..

Clearly, older ants are likely to have either been held up at congested nodes or taken a more tortuous path from their source to the destination. Relating δr to the ant's age means that these older ants will have less reinforcing effect on the routing tables of the nodes through which they pass, thus making their routes less likely to be chosen by other ants.

Testing the ABC system on a BT interconnection network (BT is the largest British telecommunications operator), and measuring its performance against that of a number of other well-known routing techniques, Schoonderwoerd et al. claimed good results. ABC's results compared with three known routing algorithms are given in Table 3.6.

Table 3.6 ABC algorithm comparative tests 1

Routing algorithm	Average call failures	Standard deviation
Shortest path	12.57	2.16
Mobile Agents	9.19	0.78
Improved Mobile Agents	4.22	0.77
ABC	1.79	0.54

There are potential problems, however, of the kind that constantly plague dynamic optimisation algorithms, as illustrated by the following question.

SAQ 3.10

Suppose a telecommunications network has gone through a long period of relative stability, with load fairly evenly balanced throughout and with all switches operating some way below their maximum capacity. What might be the effect of fierce bursts of activity flaring up in various parts of the network?

ANSWER..

The problem is that, after a long period of stability and equilibrium, the ants will have become locked into their accustomed routes. They may be unable to break out of these patterns to explore new routes capable of meeting the new conditions.

To combat this difficulty, Schoonderwoerd et al. modified the ABC algorithm by adding a noise factor g (where $0 < g < 1$). In the new version, an ant arriving at node i will choose a purely random node to visit next, with probability g. This constantly allows for the possibility of opening up new paths when the load on switches changes suddenly. Further tests on the BT network showed that ABC with added noise performed slightly worse than basic ABC in a network where the load remained fairly static. However, in tests in which the network load suddenly changed after 15,000 time steps, the results were as shown in Table 3.7.

Table 3.7 ABC algorithm comparative tests 2

Routing algorithm	Average call failures	Standard deviation
Shortest path	12.53	2.04
Mobile Agents	9.24	0.80
Improved Mobile Agents	4.41	0.85
ABC	2.72	1.24
ABC (noise)	2.56	1.05

Various improvements to Schoonderwoerd et al.'s basic model have been suggested since 1996, including:

▶ *Smart ants.* In ABC, an ant at node *i* only updates the column in *i*'s routing table that corresponds to the ant's starting node *s*. A smart ant updates the columns corresponding to every node *j* it has visited on its way from *s*, in each case by a factor based on its age when it reached *j*.

▶ *Uniform ants.* A uniform ant at node *i* will choose which of *i*'s neighbour nodes to visit next with equal probability.

Clearly ABC and its variants perform well, but they do have one severe limitation, stemming from the practicalities of real switched telecommunications networks. All these algorithms make one crucial assumption about the way a network operates. This may be rather tricky to spot, but think about this question.

Exercise 3.10

In ABC, ants and calls traverse the same links. *Calls* are routed according to their destination: the switch consults the column in its routing table and despatches the call to the neighbour node with the highest probability value. However, *ants* modify the columns in a node's routing table corresponding to their *source*: in other words, an ant is amassing information about a route backwards, as it travels from its starting point. Is the ABC system making an assumption here about the nature of the network?

Discussion ....

A call is being dispatched, say, from node *i* to node *j*. The assumption embodied in ABC is that the cost of travelling from *i* to *j* is going to be the same as travelling from *j* to *i*. In other words, the network has to be *symmetric* for the algorithm to work.

Unfortunately, although this assumption may be true of certain telephone networks, it is not necessarily true of modern, packet-switched systems. Such networks are generally asymmetric, so packets moving from a source *s* to a destination *d* may take a quite different route than they would from *d* to *s*, as illustrated in Figures 3.9 and 3.10.

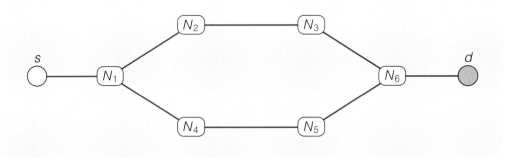

Figure 3.9   Routing in a packet-switched network

In ABC, call data are forwarded towards their *destination*, from s to d. Ants alter the routing table entries corresponding to their *source*. So in the network depicted in Figure 3.9, the ants build information about the best paths that may be quite different from the best path to be followed for the data, as shown in Figure 3.10.

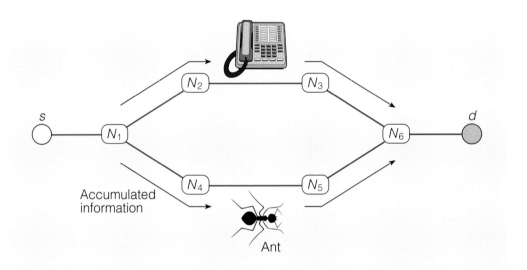

Figure 3.10   Routing in a packet switched network

A number of systems capable of dealing with both asymmetric and symmetric networks have been proposed. In one solution, every node i keeps a table that tracks the data traffic from i to all possible destinations. Ants are routed probabilistically according to this table. A more radical solution is Di Caro and Dorigo's (1998) Ant Net routing system, which has the following features:

▶ Each node i has a routing table R, as in ABC, and an additional table E of average estimated journey times to all possible destinations, together with their variances.

▶ There are two kinds of ants: forward ants, $F_{s \to d}$, and backward ants, $B_{d \to s}$.

▶ Forward ants are launched from randomly chosen starting points s towards random destinations d. A forward ant is routed from node to node towards its destination using each node's routing table, in each case choosing the neighbour with the highest probability value. As it moves it gathers information about the route it has followed and the waiting times it has encountered.

▶ When a forward ant reaches its destination, it changes to a backward ant and retraces its steps along the path it took from its source.

▶ At each node i along the return path, a backward ant $B_{d \to s}$ arriving at i makes changes to i's R and E tables. E is amended with the waiting time information the ant gathered along its route, but only good solutions are used. If the ant's trip took longer than the current best estimate, the information is discarded. R is amended by altering the entries in column d of R: the entry for the neighbour node the ant has come from is reinforced using a signal r, calculated from the ant's trip time and the estimates in E. Other values in this column are diminished by pheromone evaporation, as in Equation 3.13.

Ant Net has been tested on models of US and Japanese communications networks, using a variety of different possible traffic patterns. The algorithm worked at least as well as, and in some cases much better than, four of the best-performing conventional routing algorithms. Its results were even comparable to those of an idealised 'daemon' algorithm, with instantaneous and complete knowledge of the current state of a network.

2.4 Particle swarm optimisation (PSO)

You may remember from the case studies in Unit 1 of this block that insects are by no means the only creatures that display coordinated collective behaviour. Birds form flocks and fish swim in schools that seem ordered, but are without any central control. Particle swarm optimisation (PSO) is an optimisation technique inspired by such flocks and schools. Developed by Russell Eberhart and James Kennedy in 1995, the process was at first intended as a model of social behaviour, but it was soon applied to optimisation problems. Since then, to improve its performance, it has been repeatedly amended and developed.

Imagine the following scenario: a flock of birds is searching for a single piece of food over some large area of ground. None of the birds knows exactly where the food item is, although each one can sense how far away it is. Clearly, an effective strategy for every member of the flock is to fly towards the bird which is nearest to the food. The original PSO algorithm was based on exactly this strategy. A set of potential solutions, called particles, is created. In the case of an optimisation problem such as TSP, each particle (solution) would be a possible path through the network. Each particle then 'flies' through the solution space in a direction and at a speed that is determined by the behaviour of its neighbours and its own past performance. Figure 3.11 illustrates part of a typical two-dimensional solution space through which eight particles are flying.

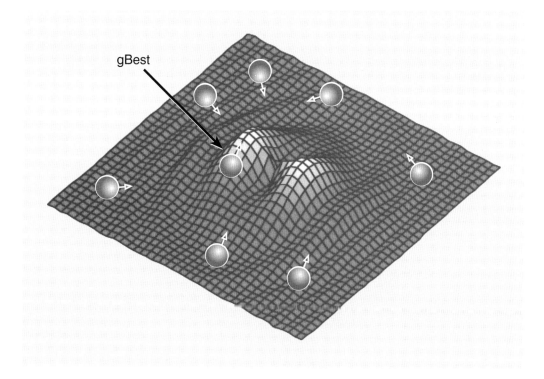

Figure 3.11　A particle swarm converging on the best solution to an optimisation problem

As with the kinds of search space you looked at in Block 2, the space can be thought of as a landscape, with hills and valleys, and with the height of any point in the space representing how good the solution at that point is, a property that we will call the solution's *fitness*. You can see that the particle marked gBest in Figure 3.11 is closest to the fittest solution in the whole landscape, and is marked as the global best.

The PSO system evolves across a number of time steps, with particles moving across the landscape seeking out better and better solutions. A particle *i* will have the following characteristics:

▶ Each particle *i* has a current *position*, represented by a vector $\mathbf{x}_i$.

▶ Since each particle *i* is moving, it has a *velocity*, represented by a vector $\mathbf{v}_i$.

▶ Each particle remembers the position at which it had its fittest result (its personal best, $\mathbf{p}_i$); this gets updated every time the particle finds a new and better solution.

▶ As they move, the particles cooperate, by exchanging information; in the basic version of PSO, each particle has a neighbourhood and knows the fitness of the particles in this neighbourhood.

▶ Each particle uses the position $\mathbf{p}_g$ of the particle in its neighbourhood with best fitness to adjust its velocity.

A neighbourhood does not have to be simply a geographical one, as illustrated in Figure 3.12. It may be defined as a social neighbourhood, comprising particles of a similar type, or simply the whole solution space – the global neighbourhood.

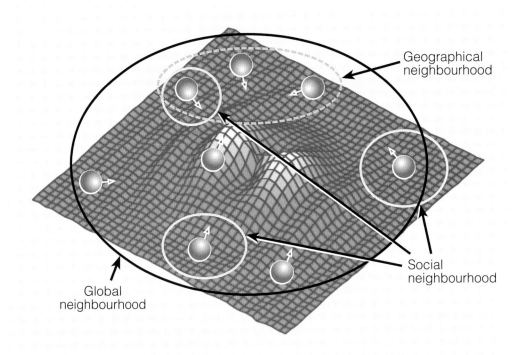

Figure 3.12　Particle swarm neighbourhoods

At each time step, all particles move to a new position, using the following equations:

$$\mathbf{v}'_i = \mathbf{v}_i + \varphi_1 \cdot (\mathbf{p}_i - \mathbf{x}_i) + \varphi_2 \cdot (\mathbf{p}_g - \mathbf{x}_i) \tag{3.15}$$

$$\mathbf{x}'_i = \mathbf{x}_i + \mathbf{v}'_i \tag{3.16}$$

where $\mathbf{v}'_i$ is the particle's new velocity, $\mathbf{x}'_i$ is its new position, and φ_1 and φ_2, are parameters. You should be able to see from Equations 3.15 and 3.16 that the adjustment to the velocity and position is basically worked out by:

▶ calculating the new velocity by adding to the current velocity a randomly weighted portion in the direction of its personal best, and a randomly weighted portion in the direction of the neighbourhood best;

▶ calculating the new position by adding the new velocity to the old position.

In the original version of the heuristic, a V_{max} parameter was implemented in order to encourage convergence. Particles' velocities were clamped to below a maximum velocity V_{max}. However, it was also reported by Shi and Eberhart that systems with this parameter typically still suffered from poor convergence towards the optima during the later stages of the algorithm's run.

The way particles adjust their positions has sometimes been called a 'psychosocial compromise': that is, it is a compromise between the individual's beliefs (the particle's personal best) and the opinions of the wider society (the neighbourhood global best). Figure 3.13 expresses this idea diagrammatically.

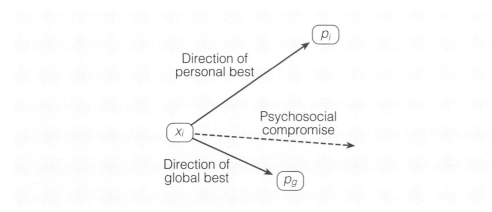

Figure 3.13   Psychosocial compromise in PSO

The pseudo-code for the basic PSO algorithm is as follows:

```
to setup
      cct N [initialise_particle]   ;; creates and initialises N particles
end
to go
    ask turtles [move_particle] ;; move every particle
end                              ;; stop at some termination condition
to move_particle
    calculate_fitness_value;
    if (fitness_value > pBest)
      [set pBest fitness_value]
    if (fitness_value > gBest)
      [set gBest fitness_value]
    calculate_velocity          ;; using Equation 3.15
    update_particle_position    ;; using Equation 3.16
  end
```

Now attempt the following exercise.

Exercise 3.11

Consider a PSO particle flying through a two-dimensional problem space. At time t the particle has the following properties:

$$\mathbf{x}_i = \begin{bmatrix} 4 \\ 7 \end{bmatrix}, \quad \mathbf{v}_i = \begin{bmatrix} 1.6 \\ 0.4 \end{bmatrix}, \quad \mathbf{p}_i = \begin{bmatrix} 16 \\ 12 \end{bmatrix}, \quad \mathbf{p}_g = \begin{bmatrix} 18 \\ 11 \end{bmatrix}$$

and the two constants are $\varphi_1 = 0.3$ and $\varphi_2 = 0.2$. What will the particle's position $\mathbf{x}'_i$ be at the next time step $t + 1$?

Discussion ....

This is a simple matter of applying Equations 3.15 and 3.16 to these vectors. (Look in the Maths Guide for the course if you're unsure about adding and subtracting vectors.)

$$\mathbf{v}'_i = \begin{bmatrix} 1.6 \\ 0.4 \end{bmatrix} + 0.3\left(\begin{bmatrix} 16 \\ 12 \end{bmatrix} - \begin{bmatrix} 4 \\ 7 \end{bmatrix}\right) + 0.2\left(\begin{bmatrix} 18 \\ 11 \end{bmatrix} - \begin{bmatrix} 4 \\ 7 \end{bmatrix}\right)$$

$$= \begin{bmatrix} 1.6 \\ 0.4 \end{bmatrix} + 0.3\begin{bmatrix} 12 \\ 5 \end{bmatrix} + 0.2\begin{bmatrix} 14 \\ 4 \end{bmatrix}$$

$$= \begin{bmatrix} 1.6 \\ 0.4 \end{bmatrix} + \begin{bmatrix} 3.6 \\ 1.5 \end{bmatrix} + \begin{bmatrix} 2.8 \\ 0.8 \end{bmatrix}$$

$$= \begin{bmatrix} 8.0 \\ 2.7 \end{bmatrix}$$

$$\mathbf{x}'_i = \begin{bmatrix} 4 \\ 7 \end{bmatrix} + \begin{bmatrix} 8.0 \\ 2.7 \end{bmatrix}$$

$$= \begin{bmatrix} 12.0 \\ 9.7 \end{bmatrix}$$

If you sketch $\mathbf{x}_i$, $\mathbf{x}'_i$, $\mathbf{p}_i$ and $\mathbf{p}_g$ on a two-dimensional space, you'll see that the particle shifts its position in the direction of a compromise between $\mathbf{p}_i$ and $\mathbf{p}_g$.

Applied to optimisation problems, the original PSO heuristic had a number of shortcomings, including the fact that:

▶ the swarm converges too quickly, making it susceptible to local optima: particles cluster into an area of solution space containing relatively good solutions which are nevertheless not the best possible;

▶ the swarm stagnates at this point: clustered around the local optimum, it fails to make further improvements although further improvements are still possible.

You will recognise these by now as typical problems of any optimisation system.

So there have been many major developments of the original heuristic – mathematical improvements that address these shortcomings. It would take up too much space to describe these in any detail. Very briefly, though, some of the following possibilities have been investigated:

▶ *Inertia weight.* In the later stages of the algorithm's run, particles which were not the global best were effectively oscillating between their previous best, and the best of the population, rather than being 'attracted' to the global best. An inertia weight includes the particle's previous velocity in Equation 3.15, introducing a tendency for a particle to continue to travel in the direction in which it was travelling.

▶ *Swarm size.* There has been some measure of success with systems in which the size of the swarm varies dynamically as the optimisation proceeds. Particles that are doing badly are persuaded to 'die', while the more successful ones give rise to clones of themselves, which then set out on new paths of exploration.

▶ *Adaptive coefficients.* Look back at Equation 3.15 and note the two coefficients φ_1 and φ_2. You'll recall that the first of these, φ_1, biases the change in velocity towards the particle's personal best; the second, φ_2, biases the change in velocity towards the global best particle. Some researchers have experimented with the algorithm so as to allow the value of each of these coefficients gradually to change as the optimisation proceeds. The better a single particle's personal best becomes, in comparison to the global best, the greater becomes the value of φ_1; the better the best particle in a particle's neighbourhood becomes, the greater becomes the value of φ_2, biasing the change in velocity towards gBest.

The PSO paradigm has been systematically tested against common benchmarks and been applied to a number of difficult optimisation problems. It has been particularly successful in training the weights of neural networks, the principles of which you will study in Block 4, performing as effectively as the usual conventional neural network training methods. PSO also does well in comparison to evolutionary computing methods, which we cover in Block 5.

PSO is an extremely simple algorithm that seems to be effective for optimising a wide range of functions. Eberhart and Kennedy view it as a form of biologically inspired computing, occupying a midway point in nature between evolutionary search, which requires millions of years, and neural interaction, which occurs on millisecond timescales. Like ACO and other swarm techniques, it is dependent on stochastic processes. Such social behaviour can be found everywhere in the animal kingdom, and one of its most useful features is that it optimises; so a good way to solve engineering optimisation problems is to model social behaviour. It is yet another example of interaction and emergence at work.

2.5 Other applications of swarm concepts

Concepts taken from the study of social insects such as ants have most successfully been applied to optimisation problems, and have generally been based on such insects' foraging behaviour. However, there is plenty of scope for examining other aspects of insect life and using ideas from these to tackle some of the other kinds of problems requiring intelligent solutions.

Exercise 3.12

Quickly look back at some of the descriptions of social insect behaviour in Units 1 and 2 of this block. What other kind of collective activities are such insects capable of? What problems could these be applied to?

Discussion ....

I noticed two related accomplishments: building and cooperative transport of materials. You saw in Unit 1, Case Study 1.6, that paper wasps build elaborate structures and manage impressive feats of cooperation and coordination to achieve these. Another feature of insect swarms and colonies, not covered in the units above, is that of *brood sorting* and *cemeteries*, where worker insects sort eggs and larvae into separate areas of the nest (brood sorting) and clear dead colony members into neat piles (cemeteries) for later disposal.

There is no space for more than a brief summary of the possibilities here. I'll conclude this section with three case studies examining practical computer models of insect building, transport abilities and brood sorting. At the time of writing, these are all active areas of research: we've included links and commentaries on the course website and/or the course DVD, if you wish to follow any of these up.

Case Study 3.2: Self-assembly

Social insects are often great builders. We've already examined the case of nest building in paper wasps; but termites, in particular, also construct large and highly structured nests, with many internal chambers, and elaborate ventilation systems providing an even temperature throughout the interior. As you learned, such building activities appear to be achieved by a combination of direct (pheromonal) or indirect (stigmergic) interaction among the insects, and between the insects and their environment. You may get a slightly deeper insight into the detailed mechanisms involved in insect construction from the following exercise.

Computer Exercise 3.2

Complete Computer Exercise 3.2 on the course DVD.

Exercise 3.13

Quickly summarise the process through which the termite colony is able to accumulate the woodchips into piles.

Discussion ....

As in all the case studies of social insect behaviour we've met previously, every agent follows a set of simple rules. In the absence of a stimulus it wanders randomly. If it bumps into a wood chip, it picks the chip up, and goes on wandering randomly until it bumps into another wood chip, at which point it puts its chip down as near as possible to the chip it has just bumped into.

This is a pretty simplified model of insect construction – as I said earlier, termite nests can be immensely elaborate – but it is a useful starting point. Note that there are no pheromones involved here: the interaction between the insects is purely stigmergic. In fact, the rule by which each simulated insect operates can be stated in general form as follows:

```
if [environment_state[X]]
    drop_chip;
```

where environment_state[X] simply means that the insect senses a certain configuration of chips around it. In the case of the simulation you've just looked at, this is just the presence of at least one chip directly in front of the agent. However, there is no reason why the configuration might not be more complex than this. For example, Figure 3.14 shows pictorially a more elaborate example of such a rule. From now on, I will refer to this kind of rule as a **microrule**. Microrules could of course be extended to three dimensions, with the insect aware of the presence of patterns of chips above and below it, as well as to its right and left.

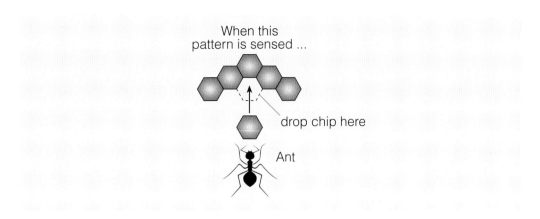

When this
pattern is sensed ...

drop chip here

Ant

Figure 3.14   An example of a microrule

The algorithm each simulated insect is following can be stated in its most general terms
as:

to move ant
    if (holding_chip)
      [apply_microrule]
    if not holding_chip **and** chip_sensed
      [pickup_chip]
    wander;
end

Each different microrule, applied over and over in this way, will lead to a different
structure. Since, obviously, the number of possible microrules is huge, so is the number
of possible structures that would be generated by this algorithm. However, pause to
think about this question for a moment.

SAQ 3.11

What do you think would be the effect of just one insect applying the above algorithm, as
against many? What might be the effect of many insects working to produce a very
complex pattern?

ANSWER...

There is no reason why one insect on its own should not produce exactly the same
structure as a swarm, only more slowly. You might have experimented with this in the
termite simulation: reducing the number of termites to just one still results in the same
piling we observe with a hundred or more.

But the piles produced in the termite simulation were just unstructured clumps of chips.
The effect of many insects working to build a more complicated and patterned structure
might be disruptive. In the simulation, it doesn't matter whether an insect removes a chip
that is already in a pile: eventually, it will be returned or placed in another pile. However,
in an intricate and ordered pattern, the work of one insect may all too easily be disrupted
by the actions of another, arriving later. The result would most likely be chaos, not order.

Simulations show that the great majority of the structures produced by the algorithm are
indeed completely uninteresting – simply amorphous shapes that fill up space, nothing
like the functional, regular patterns we see in insect constructions. However, Theraulaz
and Bonabeau have shown that a small class of algorithms based on the one described
above, called **coordinated algorithms**, do produce clearly ordered structures, similar
to those found in nature. In coordinated algorithms, the building period is divided into
separate, non-overlapping phases: microrules used in one phase do not apply in

another. You may remember from Case Study 1.6 in Unit 1 that exactly this sort of abrupt switching of behaviour occurred in the building of the paper wasp nest.

There is a great deal of interest today, among nanotechnologists, engineers, roboticists and architects, in self-assembling structures. So far, the application of swarm intelligence strategies to this problem is in its infancy. Research continues.

Case Study 3.3: Collective transport

Many species of social insects work cooperatively to carry large prey items back to their nests. An ant on its own can generally carry up to five times its own weight; but prey such as grasshoppers, spiders, cockroaches or earthworms may weigh hundreds, or even thousands of times as much as this. In many cases such items are sawn up and transported back piecemeal. However, a cooperative approach is often taken to move the prey back in one piece. A group of about a hundred ants of the species *Pheidologeton diversus* has been observed to carry a 10-centimetre earthworm weighing 1.92 grams (5000 times the weight of a single ant). In laboratory experiments with the same species, a group of fourteen ants were able to carry a piece of cereal which, if broken up, would have required 498 ants to move it piecemeal.

The process by which ants collaborate to move large objects is, inevitably, complex and ill understood. Although it is difficult to generalise across species, it seems to follow the following pattern:

1   A scouting ant will first try to move the object on its own. If it cannot lift the object, the ant will try to drag it. If this fails, it will try dragging at various different angles. The time the ant spends trying to move the object on its own seems to depend on the object's weight, and may vary from one to four minutes.

2   Eventually the scout gives up and recruits other ants by releasing a chemical secretion into the air. Only nestmates less than 2 metres away are able to sense this. If this strategy does not attract enough helpers the scout lays a chemical trail from the prey to the nest. When enough ants have been recruited, any surplus ones return to the nest. The number of ants that become involved appears to be directly proportional to the weight of the object.

3   How the ants coordinate their movement of the object is not properly understood, but is definitely not mediated by pheromones. If the prey item will not move, individual ants will apply force at various different angles. If this fails, the ants rearrange themselves around the perimeter of the prey until it starts to budge. The behaviour of one ant with respect to the object and the position and resistance of the object itself seem to modify the behaviour of other group members, causing them to change their orientation or position. This is a classic example of stigmergy.

4   If the group succeeds in carrying a prey item in one direction it continues to move it in that direction. At this point, recruitment stops.

A number of robotic systems based on models of ants' collective transport capabilities have been developed. One impressive example originated from the Collective Robotics Research Project at the University of Alberta, constructed by Kube and Bonabeau (2000). In Kube's experiments a group of up to six wheeled robots, each about 20 centimetres wide, collaborated in pushing boxes of various sizes around an area of the laboratory. In a set of demonstrations of increasing complexity, the robots were able to:

▶ arrange themselves in such a way that the box was moved in a single direction;

▶ move the box cooperatively towards a specific goal position;

▶ move the box cooperatively to a sequence of goal positions.

The internal details of this type of robot need not concern us now: it's a subject I will touch on in the next unit. For the moment, two details are worth mentioning:

▶ There was no direct communication between the robots. Each machine responded stigmergically only to changes in the environment.

▶ Internally, the robots had no world model and no explicit representational system. The behaviour of each simply arose from interactions between a set of simple, low-level behaviours.

Figure 3.15 shows snapshots of Kube's team of robots pushing a box towards a brightly lit goal. You can also watch a short but entertaining video of them at work; see the course DVD for details.

Fig 3.15   A swarm of six robots join forces to push a box towards a brightly lit goal

Swarm robotics is now a major research area. Although there has been a lot of successful work on robotic *teams* (the Robo cup, for instance), a robotic swarm is rather a different conception. In a robotic swarm system, the robots should be:

▶ numerous – perhaps between 10^2 and 10^{22} (!) individuals;

▶ homogenous – there should be only a very few different types, preferably only one type;

▶ simple – the robots will only have a very limited range of behaviours;

▶ locally aware – they will only be able to sense their immediate environment and communicate over short distances.

The inspiration from insect colonies is obvious here.

Case Study 3.4: Brood sorting and cemetery organisation

In the description of the nest-building habits of paper wasps in Unit 1, Case Study 1.6, I mentioned in passing that groups of wasps take on the task of cleaning the nest and removing the corpses of dead nestmates. Such activity is common among social insects. Some species, however, demonstrate a rather more elaborate approach to their dead. The ant species *Lasius niger* and *Messor sancta*, among others, form cemeteries of dead nestmates, by arranging their bodies in neat piles: exactly how and why they do so is unclear, although the process is undoubtedly stigmergic, similar to the one you came across in the termite building simulation. Even more intriguingly, the ant *Leptothorax unifasciatus* has been observed to sort its brood into neat patterns, with eggs clustered closely together in the innermost area, and surrounded by concentric rings of prepupae and larvae, at increasing distance. The further the brood are from the centre, the more space each individual has to itself. Experiments demonstrate that the amount of space available to each individual in its ring is proportional not to its size, but to its metabolic rate.

In a classic work of 1994, Lumer and Faieta applied this concept to the traditional computing problems of **data analysis** and **data mining**. Here is a quick outline of how their procedure works. Consider a bank with a database of customer details. For simplicity's sake, let's imagine the bank is only interested in three of the attributes of each customer: age, income and average balance. Now it is often useful for organisations to explore the ways in which the data in their databases clusters together, possibly so as to relate these clusters to other attributes. For instance, using our banking example, three customers:

Bloggs (18; 22 467; −419)

Lovejoy (19; 23 000; −499)

Dobbyn (17; 20 000; −554)

are all obviously close together, as the values of each of their three attributes (in brackets) are all very similar. In contrast:

Gates (50; 1 239 000; +8 000)

clearly doesn't belong to this group. Now we can imagine the bank's customers being distributed in a three-dimensional space (one dimension for each of the three attributes). Every object in this space can be said to be a certain *distance* from the others. Obviously Bloggs and Lovejoy are close together; Bloggs and Gates are far apart. There are various ways of measuring distances, but I don't propose to go into these here: I will just refer to the distance between two objects o_i and o_j as $d(o_i, o_j)$ and the space in which they are distributed as the **space of attributes** S. Clearly then, Bloggs, Lovejoy and Dobbyn will form a cluster in S, as in Figure 3.16.

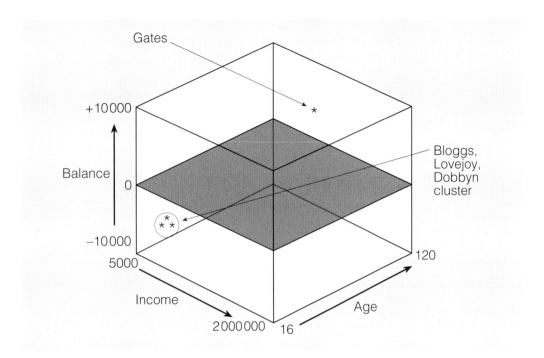

Figure 3.16 Three-dimensional space of attributes

This sort of clustering information can be very useful, particularly in the targeting of the bank's services. However, you can see that it can all become very complex: a bank with data on fifty attributes of each customer will be looking for clusters in a fifty-dimensional space of attributes. Don't imagine that mathematicians are any better at picturing such a space than you are: it is quite impossible to visualise. So the mining problem here is not just to find the clusters themselves, but to transform the results into a picture that can be visualised, usually a two-dimensional one. We call this picture the **space of representation**.

Lumer and Faieta (1994) tackled the problem using an ant colony model. Initially, data objects are deposited randomly across a two-dimensional grid (the space of representation). Virtual ants move around the grid, with each able to see a small neighbourhood N of n squares around its present position. Each ant proceeds as follows:

▶ If an empty-handed ant encounters an object o_i, it examines all the objects o_j in the n elements of N around o_i. It then calculates the local density $f(o_i)$ of objects around o_i using the following formula:

$$f(o_i) = \max\left\{0, \frac{1}{n}\sum_{o_j \in N} 1 - \frac{d(o_i, o_j)}{\alpha}\right\}$$ (3.17)

where α is a constant. Note that the measure $d(o_i, o_j)$ is a measurement of the distance in the space of attributes, *not* the space of representation. You can also see that if there are no objects around o_i, the local density will be 0.

▶ The ant then uses $f(o_i)$ to calculate a probability p_p that it will pick up o_i, using the formula:

$$p_\mu \quad \left(\frac{k_p}{k_p + f(o_i)}\right)$$ (3.18)

where k_p is a constant. If o_i is very similar to its surrounding objects, there is a high probability it will be left where it is; if it is very dissimilar, it will probably be picked up. If there are no neighbours, the probability that o_i will be picked up is 1.

▶ When an ant that is carrying o_i reaches a vacant site, it makes the same calculation of $f(o_i)$ for the neighbourhood of that site, and then works out the probability that it will drop the object by applying:

$$p_d = \begin{cases} 2f(o_i) & \text{if } f(o_i) < k_d \\ 1 & \text{otherwise} \end{cases}$$

(3.19)

where k_d is a constant. If there are no neighbours, the probability that o_i will be dropped is 0.

Lumer and Faieta applied this algorithm to a specimen bank database of 1650 customers, using a variety of distance measures to calculate $d(o_i, o_j)$, and obtained significant clustering. Their algorithm has been the basis of much further work, with applications to data retrieval, document analysis, image retrieval, architecture and World Wide Web usage mining. You can find further information on the course DVD.

3 Conclusions – swarm intelligence

Now is the time to wrap up this unit. I've looked in some depth at some of the theory of how a kind of collective intelligence can arise in swarms, and at some of the areas in which this intelligence can be put to use. Let's conclude with a final exercise.

Exercise 3.14

What do you think might be the general advantages of using a swarm of virtual agents, or a swarm of real, physical robots, in certain kinds of problem solving? Could there be disadvantages?

Discussion ....

There are no win–win solutions in computing. Everything we try always involves a trade-off of some kind. So while there are many good reasons for adopting a swarm strategy for certain kinds of problem, such an approach can introduce new problems as well. I thought that among these might be some of the advantages:

▶ Some tasks may be too difficult for a single robot to perform on its own, either because they are too complex or because they require more power than a lone robot could muster.

▶ Tasks might be performed much faster by a group of agents or robots.

▶ It is likely to be easier, and it may be more economical, to design and build a collection of simple agents or robots.

▶ A swarm of simple robots is likely to be more robust and flexible than a single, very complex one. If one member of the set breaks down (which is less likely anyway, if each robot is simple) then this probably won't affect the collective behaviour very much. And we've seen many times above that the random fluctuations that can be built into swarm behaviour protect the group against stagnation.

▶ A swarm system is typically *decentralised*: it has no master controller. This cuts out the need for a lot of expensive and time-wasting communication between the individual agents and central command, which again makes the system more robust – a centrally controlled system will break down entirely if the central controller breaks down.

But there are disadvantages too, including these:

▶ Swarm systems can easily become stagnated into inefficient solutions or behaviour. As you've seen, a lot of ingenuity has to be spent on tuning the system's behaviour so as to strike a balance between rapidly converging on a solution and exploring new paths.

▶ Because the behaviour we want to coax out of the swarm is emergent, we can't directly deduce from the behaviour of the individuals in the swarm exactly what this behaviour will be (look back at our discussion of emergence in Unit 2, Section 2.2, if you are uncertain about this point). Consequently, swarm systems are difficult to program and may require a lot of tuning before they perform well.

As you saw in Unit 2 of this block, interaction and emergence do not only occur in swarms. Complex behaviour can also arise from these mechanisms in individual, solitary agents. This will be the theme of the next unit.

Summary of Unit 3

In this unit I have concentrated on interaction and emergence in swarms of simple agents. First, I explored at some length the principles of ant colony optimisation, in which swarms of virtual 'insects' interact to tackle optimisation problems, as well as other tasks requiring 'intelligent' solutions, such as self-assembly, collective transport and data mining. I showed how positive and negative feedback and the amplification of random fluctuations could lead the colony into emergent solutions to such problems. I outlined the ACO metaheuristic and presented several ant systems that are variations on this basic theme. A case study demonstrated how ant colony techniques could be applied to the dynamic optimisation of telecommunications networks, as well as to other significant problems in engineering, data analysis and design.

More briefly, and by way of contrast, I discussed particle swarm optimisation, another form of biologically inspired computing based on the social interactions of animals and humans. We showed how, in PSO, the interaction of swarms of elementary 'particles' can also cause solutions to optimisation problems to emerge.

For now, though, look back at the learning outcomes for this unit and check these against what you think you can now do. Return to any section of the unit if you need to.

Unit 4: Interaction, emergence, adaptation and selection in individuals

CONTENTS

1	Introduction to Unit 4		116
	What you need to study this unit		116
	Learning outcomes for Unit 4		117
2	Interaction and emergence – reactive robotics		118
	2.1	Robotics – the ethological background	121
	2.2	Interaction and emergence in robotics	123
3	Adaptation and selection		146
	3.1	What is learned?	148
	3.2	How is learning brought about?	149
	3.3	What adapts?	152
	3.4	Learning through evolution	157
4	Coda: Artificial life? Living computers?		162
	4.1	What is artificial life?	162
	4.2	DNA and molecular computing	163
5	Summary of Unit 4		164
	References and further reading		167
	Acknowledgements		169
	Index for Block 3		170

Introduction to Unit 4

In the previous unit, I looked in detail at how ordered behaviour arises in a swarm of simple individuals, as an emergent property of interactions among its members. I tried to show how this behaviour can be modelled and the models applied to solve hard problems in optimisation, data mining, collective transport and construction. However, as you know from Unit 2, interaction and emergence do not only happen in swarms. Ordered behaviour can also emerge in agents acting alone, as a result of:

▶ interactions between the individual and its environment;

▶ interactions within the individual.

In this last unit of Block 3, I want to follow up on these two kinds of interaction. I also want to give you an idea of how adaptation and selection, which will play such a large part in Blocks 4 and 5, may fit into the picture. Firstly, we'll look at interaction and emergence in individuals by considering how the two forms of interaction above come together in a field of research known as **reactive robotics**. I'll then discuss how robots and other systems may be capable of adaptation, and offer examples of some of the forms such adaptation might take. Finally, I will offer a detailed case study which I think indicates how the principle of selection can be made to work.

What you need to study this unit

You will need the following course components, and will need to use your computer and internet connection for some of the exercises.

▶ this Block 3 text

▶ the course DVD.

LEARNING OUTCOMES FOR UNIT 4

After studying this unit you will be able to:

4.1 write a short paragraph distinguishing between conventional SENSE–PLAN–ACT and reactive SENSE–ACT approaches to robotics;

4.2 explain some of the key ethological concepts underlying reactive robotics;

4.3 write a detailed explanation, with illustrations, of subsumption architectures;

4.4 write a detailed explanation, with illustrations, of potential fields strategies;

4.5 list the main approaches to adaptation in modern robotic and agent systems;

4.6 write a brief explanation of the role of evolution in recent adaptive systems;

4.7 suggest brief definitions of artificial life and molecular computing.

2 Interaction and emergence – reactive robotics

You will recall from Block 2 and Unit 2 of this block that there was much talk of robots. There are a number of reasons for this: at present, research into intelligent robots is a booming field; there is an ever-growing demand for ever more intelligent and independent robots; and, as I suggested in Block 1, much of the future of AI research may lie in robotics. In this section I am going to try to expand this discussion and present some of the principles of current robotic research in a rather more formal and systematic way.

But why do we need robots? Practically speaking, the answer lies in a rather overworked maxim roboticists use when justifying their work: the three Ds – Dirty, Dull, Dangerous. Machines have no finer feelings, so there can be no problem in employing them in work that humans are reluctant to carry out, such as sewer exploration and cleaning. Machines don't get bored, so using them for time-consuming, repetitive jobs, such as assembly line work is a logical move: they will continue to work tirelessly and accurately long after humans would have become so exhausted and jaded that they are making constant mistakes. And robots can work in environments that would mean immediate death to humans.

SAQ 4.1

Think of a few more examples of dirty, dull and dangerous jobs which would be ideal for robots.

ANSWER...

Dirty jobs could include cleaning and agriculture. Among the dull jobs suitable for robots is industrial assembly, an area where robots have been used for many years. Dangerous jobs might include space exploration, maintenance and repair of nuclear reactors and undersea work.

Here are two real examples of current work.

Case Study 4.1: LEMUR

NASA JPL has developed a small, six-legged walking robot, LEMUR (see Figure 4.1), weighing less than 5 kg, designed to have the agility and skill to carry out small-scale assembly, inspection and maintenance tasks in space. NASA describes LEMUR as having 'Swiss Army knife tendencies': it has six fully independent limbs, each of which can be configured to carry a variety of different tools for inspection and manipulation, including grippers, ball-drivers and a camera.

Figure 4.1   LEMUR robot climbing a steeply sloping wall

However, robotic research may have uses other than the immediately practical: building robots based on biological principles can also help us to a better understanding of how animals perceive and manipulate the world, and of animal intelligence generally. Such systems are generally termed **biomimetic** (mimicking life). There is a fruitful dialogue to be had here between biologists and robot engineers.

Case Study 4.2: Lobster robot

The biomimetic robot illustrated in Figure 4.2 was developed at the Marine Science Center at Northeastern University, USA. An eight-legged device, it is firmly modelled on the sensory and ambulatory patterns of the lobster, and is intended as a prototype for a series of devices for exploration of the ocean bottom.

Figure 4.2   Lobster robot

Industrial robots have been in use for several decades now, on assembly lines and in other automated factories. An industrial robot is described in the ISO Standard 8373:1994 as an 'automatically controlled, reprogrammable, multipurpose manipulator programmable in three or more axes'. Most industrial robots are robot arms programmed to carry out specific actions over and over again without variation but with great precision. Some have rather more flexibility than this: they may be linked to machine vision subsystems acting as their 'eyes', which enable them to position themselves accurately in relation to the object they are handling. But, although present-day industrial robots are superb engineering achievements, they are not what we are interested in here. Nor am I going to consider telerobots, machines controlled by human operators, generally across great distances. NASA's Sojourner, which explored the surface of Mars from July to September 1997, was an example of such a telerobot. My focus here is on **autonomous** or **intelligent** robots.

Wikipedia has this to say about autonomous robots:

> Autonomous robots are robots which can perform desired tasks in unstructured environments without continuous human guidance ... Different robots can be autonomous in different ways. A high degree of autonomy is particularly desirable in fields such as space exploration, where communication delays and interruptions are unavoidable.

Source: www.wikipedia.org

As I pointed out in Unit 2, even quite simple animals are capable of a high degree of autonomy and are able to negotiate complex, hostile and dynamic environments with apparent ease. After all, they have evolved to do just this. So it makes sense to take the same line as the Marine Science Center and seek to understand animal capacities and simulate them in robotic systems. Let's start, then, with a quick look at the ethological background to modern robotics.

2.1 Robotics – the ethological background

Just to get us started, consider this simple question.

SAQ 4.2

What is ethology?

ANSWER...

As you learned in Unit 1, ethology is the study of the behaviour of animals in their natural environment. For most ethologists this would also include the study of animals under conditions of domestication or in the laboratory to confirm field observations.

Although the study of animal behaviour can be traced back to Darwin and before, the founders of modern ethology are generally reckoned to be Konrad Lorenz and Niko Tindbergen. Lorenz originated the idea of the **fixed action patterns** (FAPs), which he defined as instinctive responses that occur reliably when a definite stimulus is presented to an animal. He called this the **sign stimulus** or **releasing stimulus** and was able to show that important forms of animal communication arise from the combination of a few simple FAPs. Lorenz's second major discovery was **imprinting**, a process in which the behaviours that certain animals are born with, such as the tendency of tern chicks to peck at the red spot at the base of their mother's beak, can be transferred to a different stimulus, such as the end of a red pencil. Tindbergen directed the gaze of ethologists towards four aspects of animal behaviour:

▶ its effect on the animal's chances of survival and reproduction;

▶ the stimuli that cause the behaviour;

▶ how the behaviour changes as the animal ages and develops;

▶ how the behaviour compares with that of related species.

Both men, and all ethologists subsequently, place the idea of a **behaviour** at the forefront of their thinking. Following Lorenz, we can define a behaviour as a reliable association between a certain sensory stimulus and a fixed pattern of motor response. To take one of the examples from Unit 1, if a lobster senses a certain configuration of chemicals in a plume, this activates a series of muscle movements that will propel it towards (or away from) the plume's source. The stimulus that fires the motor action is the releasing stimulus.

Not all behaviours follow this simple stimulus–response pattern, of course. Ethologists classify behaviours into three categories:

▶ *Reflexive*. These are the kind of reflex responses found in creatures such as insects. The animal responds directly to a stimulus with a motor pattern and without any intervening processing. The building activities of paper wasps are clear examples of this, as is the tendency of moths to fly towards a light. Higher mammals such as humans have numerous reflexes, such as the reaction of the pupils to light.

▶ *Reactive*. Unlike reflexes, which are innate, reactive behaviours are learned but behave rather like reflexes, in that no deliberation comes between the stimulus and the response. Good examples include the ability of terns to navigate by star patterns and herring gulls to recognise good dropping zones for their prey. Similarly, bees appear to learn the landmarks around their hive.

Figure 4.3   Konrad Lorenz (top) and Niko Tindbergen (below)

▶ *Conscious.* More complex animals such as primates appear to take conscious control of some of their behaviours: they analyse stimuli, deliberate, plan and then execute responses which can be tuned with great flexibility if circumstances require. Writing this block has been a good example of a complex behaviour.

A major problem for ethologists (and for roboticists) is understanding how a number of simple behaviours can be combined and run concurrently to create more complex actions, while avoiding deadlocks and ambiguous or inappropriate responses.

SAQ 4.3

What role do you think perception plays in behaviour? Do you think the view of perception that we've presented so far is limited in any way?

ANSWER...

Perception is obviously necessary for picking up, analysing and recognising sensory stimuli, all with a view to triggering the right kind of action. But I think the above analysis of behaviour underestimates the extent to which perception also *guides* actions as they are carried out. Rather than being a simple SENSE followed by ACT sequence, most of the time behaviour and perception are locked together, each feeding back to the other.

Perception, then, plays a twofold role in behaviour:

▶ It releases a particular behaviour.

▶ It provides ongoing information on how best to carry out the behaviour.

This coupling of perception and action is generally referred to as the **perception–action cycle**, a term coined by the psychologist Ulrich Neisser. An agent perceives the world and initiates an action; this action changes the world in some way; the change is then perceived; this perception is the basis for the next phase of the action; and so on (see Figure 4.4).

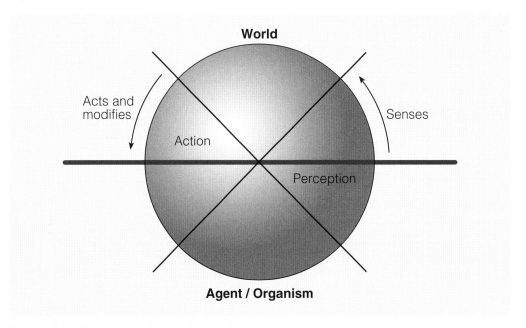

Figure 4.4   The perception–action cycle

A final, and crucial, figure in the ethological background to modern robotics is J. J. Gibson. Gibson believed psychologists and ethologists needed to make radical changes to the way they understood perception. Like Neisser, he believed that perception is designed for action – we perceive in order to *control* our environment – and that the environment presents us with directly perceivable possibilities for action, such as surfaces for walking, handles for pulling, space for navigation, tools for manipulating. He called these **affordances**. Our whole evolution, Gibson claimed, has been geared toward perceiving useful possibilities for action.

Gibson's work has been immensely influential, not only in cognitive science, but also in areas such as ergonomics and design. A collaborator and follower of his offers this definition of an affordance:

> You are approaching a door through which you eventually want to pass. The door, and the manner in which it is secured to the wall, permits opening by pushing it from its 'closed' position. We say that the door affords ... opening by pushing. On approaching that door you observe a flat plate fixed to it at waist height on the 'non-hinge' side, and possibly some sticky finger marks on its otherwise polished surface. You deduce that the door is meant to be pushed open: you therefore push on the plate, whereupon the door opens and you pass through. Here, there is a perceived affordance, triggered by the sight of the plate and the finger marks ... Note that the affordance we discuss is neither the door nor the plate: it is a property of the door ...
>
> Source: Norman (1988), p. 87

All these ethological understandings of animal behaviour have carried over into the theory and practice of modern robotics. Let's now move on to look at this theory and practice in detail.

2.2 Interaction and emergence in robotics

Think back to the robot Ambler, described in Unit 2, Section 2.1, of this block. Look back at the relevant section, if you want.

SAQ 4.4

Why was Ambler so poor at coping with the world?

ANSWER..

Ambler's problem was that it carried a symbolic map of its entire world in its 'brain'. After every movement it had to stop to consult this and to plan its next move.

Now consider this case study.

Case Study 4.3: Toto

The robot Toto was designed and built in the late 1980s by Maja Mataric, then a researcher at the MIT Robotics Laboratory. Toto's 'body' (see Figure 4.5) was a 30-centimetre cylinder mounted on a three-wheeled mobile base. Around the circumference of its body was mounted a ring of twelve ultrasonic ranging sensors. Toto was completely autonomous and free to move anywhere within the laboratory and the surrounding offices and corridors.

Figure 4.5   Toto robot

As you learned in Block 2, in conventional robotic systems the internal model is based on the *objects* to be found in the robot's 'world' – usually blocks or other simple articles – all expressed in a suitable symbolic language, and with a central planner operating on them. Toto's software was quite differently designed. It was a collection of *behaviours* or **competences** – things that the robot could *do*, each one taking information directly from sensors and feeding a suitable response directly to the **actuators** (the motors that make the robot move, manipulate things, etc.). At the lowest level, Toto had just four basic behaviours:

▶ *stroll*: in the absence of obstacles or other dangers within a certain distance, simply move forward;

▶ *avoid*: on sensing an obstacle, change the direction of travel by an angle just big enough to veer around it;

▶ *align*: while edging around the body of an object, or following a wall, change the direction of travel to prevent moving too far away;

▶ *correct*: use the side sonars to follow concave edges of objects by constantly adjusting the direction of travel.

Figure 4.6 shows how useful behaviour emerged from these four competences interacting together. Toto could move down corridors, turning where necessary, and work its way round objects. In fact, as you'll see later, Toto was also given some higher-level internal modelling competences: it was able to learn landmarks and a map of the laboratory, and it could plan paths. I'll talk about these later in the unit. However, there was no central, complete symbolic model. Memories were dynamic and activated only when they were required. There was no central planner.

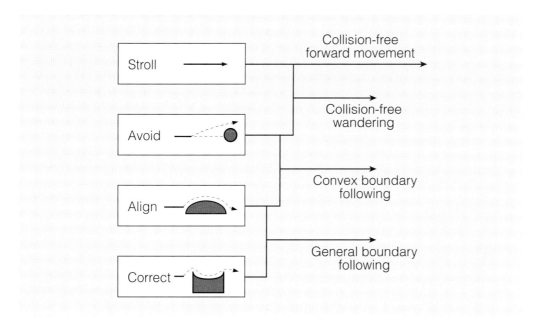

Figure 4.6   Toto's internal behaviours

SAQ 4.5

In what ways do you think Toto's internal design was inspired by insect models of behaviour?

ANSWER..

You can recognise some of the features of the cockroach and the bee. There is a close coupling between sensors and actuators, with little or no intervening deliberation or planning. Both Toto and the insects are in constant touch with their environment, perpetually sensing, responding and adjusting to it. As in the case of the honeybee (Case Study 2.3), internal memories are dynamic and only available when needed.

The director of the MIT Robotics Laboratory, Rodney Brooks, had for many years promoted a view of robotics, with implications for AI in general, that rejected internal models and the SENSE–PLAN–ACT cycle. Brooks argued that robots were of no use unless they could operate successfully in real environments – crowded buildings, cluttered offices, areas full of moving objects – and that no conventional robot had any prospect of succeeding in this. Instead, Brooks urged a parsimonious approach, based on the capabilities of simple creatures such as insects, in which sensation, action and environment are closely coupled. The SENSE–PLAN–ACT cycle was to be replaced with a **SENSE–ACT cycle**. There is no need for complex internal models of the world, for – in Brooks's own words – 'the world is its own best representation'. Why represent it, when it can be accessed directly? For many years, Brooks was a lone voice, but his approach has proved immensely successful. It has come to be called **behaviour-based robotics** or **reactive robotics**.

To look a little further at the principles of reactive robotics, try to answer the following question.

SAQ 4.6

What features of Toto seem to be based on the ethological understanding of animal function that I discussed earlier?

ANSWER..

The most obvious answer is the concentration on *behaviour*. Toto's responses to the world were organised around a set of simple behaviours – stroll, avoid, align, and so on. Quite complex behaviour then *emerges* from the *interaction* between these simple response patterns.

There is a possibility of some confusion here, which at this stage I should clear up. Ethologically speaking, one would call Toto's behaviours reflexive: they are *inbuilt* and involve a direct coupling between perception and action, with no learning or reasoning involved. However, the name *reactive robotics* was originally given to Brooks's approach, and the name has stuck. But although modern roboticists are interested in learning and adaptation, as we shall see, most of the time they are dealing in behaviours that ethologists would call reflexive, rather than truly reactive. However, I will continue to use the term reactive robotics, or the more neutral *behaviour-based robotics*.

The idea of a behaviour, then, is a centrepiece of modern robotic thinking. As in ethology, a behaviour is taken to be a direct mapping between perception and action, a simple machine of the form illustrated in Figure 4.7.

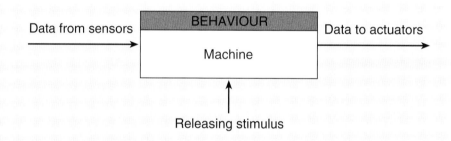

Figure 4.7   A robotic behaviour

Of course, early robots such as Shakey had behaviours too. But the key difference between reactive robots and earlier models, pointed out by Rodney Brooks, lies in the way behaviours fit together. Brooks distinguished between a **horizontal** and a **vertical decomposition** of functions inside a robot. Take a conventional robot like Ambler or Shakey. The way modules work together inside such a machine is illustrated in Figure 4.8.

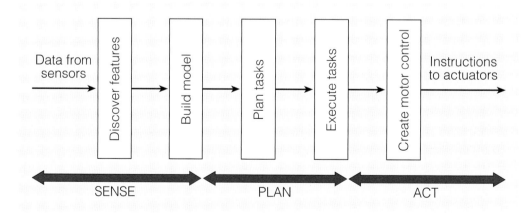

Figure 4.8   Horizontal decomposition of behaviours

It's easy to see that in this SENSE–PLAN–ACT cycle one can trace a direct line in time from sensing, through planning, to the final motor response. We have already seen some of the disadvantages of such an approach in our discussions of Ambler: it's slow; it's fragile, in the sense that if anything goes wrong anywhere in the sequence, it may not be possible to produce any response at all; and much of it may be redundant, as a lot of basic behaviour needs no elaborate planning. In contrast, Brooks pointed to the vertical decomposition characteristic of reactive robotics, as illustrated in Figure 4.9.

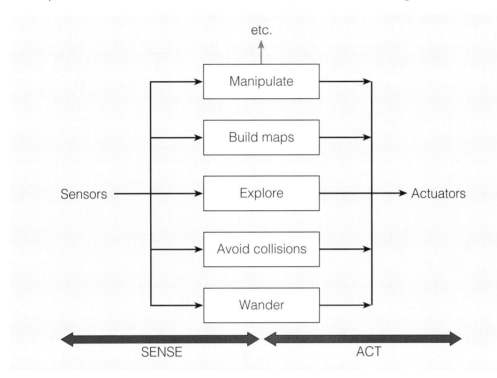

Figure 4.9   Vertical decomposition of behaviours

Note certain crucial differences between such an architecture and the horizontal one of Figure 4.8:

▶ All of the behaviours have access to the same sensor information.

▶ The behaviours work together, in parallel.

▶ Behaviours higher in the stack may use lower behaviours, inhibit them, override them or modulate them in some way.

You can probably see that such an architecture will have a number of advantages over the more traditional horizontal decomposition.

Exercise 4.1

Note down some of the possible advantages for the roboticist of a vertical architecture of behaviours.

Discussion ....

I thought of the following:

▶ *Robustness*. If a higher-level behaviour fails then the lower-level behaviours can still be counted on to produce a response.

▶ *Modularity*. Such an architecture should be easier to program.

▶ *Speed*. The parallel working of behaviours should give a speed advantage over traditional sequential architectures.

▶ *Efficiency*. Lower-level behaviours handle reflexive responses, with more elaborate planning behaviour being called in only when it is needed.

No doubt there are other advantages you may have thought of.

However, let me repeat a point I made in Unit 3 in connection with swarm systems. The behaviour of a swarm is *emergent*, so can't be directly deduced from the behaviour of the individuals that make it up. Consequently, such systems require careful programming and tuning. Vertically arranged, behaviour-based systems offer exactly the same challenge: the interaction between behaviours produces emergent behaviour in the robot, which is difficult to predict and control. Much of the work of modern robotics is devoted to evolving strategies and architectures for handling this problem. Two main approaches stand out: **subsumption architectures** and **potential fields methods**. We can now move on to look at these.

Subsumption architectures

Rodney Brooks found himself constantly at odds with other roboticists throughout the 1980s and 1990s. He believed that much of the work then going on, based on the SENSE–PLAN–ACT model, simply missed the point. The true requirements of any robot and its control system, he claimed, were:

▶ *Realism.* The robot must be able to negotiate an unpredictable, dynamic, three-dimensional physical world, containing irregular objects of varying sizes – in contrast to the carefully controlled, simplified worlds with which Shakey and its successors dealt.

▶ *Autonomy.* The robot must be able to do this without any external guidance.

▶ *Multiple goals.* The robot will have many different goals, some of which may conflict. For example, a robot assigned to inspect a railway track for cracks must be able to get out of the way of an oncoming train.

▶ *Multiple sensors.* A robot should have many sensors of different types: infrared, sonar, TV cameras, and so on. Since all of these will be inaccurate to some degree, will feed in data that overlaps with that from other sensors, and will give inconsistent readings from time to time, a means has to be found to filter and integrate all this information into a form useful to the robot. Brooks pointed to the fact that birds and insects (as you learned in Units 1 and 2) use multiple independent navigation systems.

▶ *Robustness.* If sensors or internal components fail, the robot should be able to carry on and, if possible, adapt.

▶ *Extensibility.* It should be easy to add new behaviours to the robot without damaging the capabilities it has already.

▶ *Simplicity.* Keep it simple! Complex behaviour does not necessarily mean a complex control system. Nor does it require profound mathematical analysis. Brooks rather charmingly referred to those colleagues who covered page after page of their papers with equations as suffering from 'physics envy'.

Brooks believed these goals could be met through the vertical decomposition of tasks that I illustrated above in Figure 4.9. He called each layer of the decomposition a **level of competence**. Refer back to Figure 4.9 for a minute. Brooks characterised the function of each of the layers depicted there as follows:

Level 0 causes the robot to move around aimlessly;

Level 1 makes the robot avoid bumping into things;

Level 2 detects places in the distance to visit and heads for them;

Level 3 builds maps of the robot's immediate environment;

Level 4 builds on the lower layers to enable the robot to interact purposefully with the objects it detects in its explorations.

Figure 4.10   Rodney Brooks

And so on – more and more layers can be added. You can see that in this model higher layers are dependent on lower ones. For a robot to wander it must be able to avoid collisions; to move to a new location, it must be able to wander and to avoid collisions, and so on. Brooks referred to the relationship between layers as **subsumption**: layers work in parallel and independently, but a lower layer may find that a higher layer is examining and overriding its behaviours – *subsuming* them, in Brooks's terminology.

Brooks and his MIT colleagues constructed several robots based on this subsumption architecture. Characteristically, each layer consists of a number of simple, connected modules, each on an **augmented finite state machine** (AFSM). Figure 4.11 shows a schematic picture of a typical AFSM.

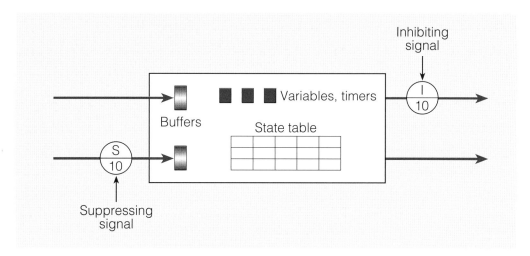

Figure 4.11   An augmented finite state machine (AFSM)

Each AFSM has the following features:

▶   a number of input lines and output lines. Input messages are buffered and can be lost if a new message arrives on the same line before the earlier message is processed;

▶   internal variables and timers;

▶   a state table, setting out a number of possible states; each state will be one of four possible types:

output: a message is sent along one of the output lines; the AFSM then makes a transition to a new state, specified in its state table;

side effect: a new value is computed for one of the internal variables; the AFSM then makes a transition to a new state, specified in its state table;

conditional dispatch: the system moves to one or another of two possible new states, based on the values of messages in the input buffers and the values of internal variables;

event dispatch: input buffers and timers are monitored until certain conditions are met, whereupon the AFSM makes a transition to a new state, specified in its state table;

▶   messages along input lines that can be *suppressed* and along output lines that can be *inhibited* by messages from AFSMs in a higher layer (this is subsumption). Suppression means that the input is *replaced* by another message, for a specified length of time; inhibition means that the outgoing message is *delayed* for a specified length of time. The timings involved are indicated by the numbers in Figure 4.11.

To see how these machines fit together within and between layers, we can consider a robot constructed by Brooks's group in 1986 and described in a classic paper. The Level 0 layer consists of six AFSMs, one of which, SONAR, is connected to all of the robot's twelve sonar sensors and two of which, TURN and FORWARD, are connected directly to its drive mechanism. The remaining three modules are purely internal. The complete architecture of Level 0 is represented in Figure 4.12.

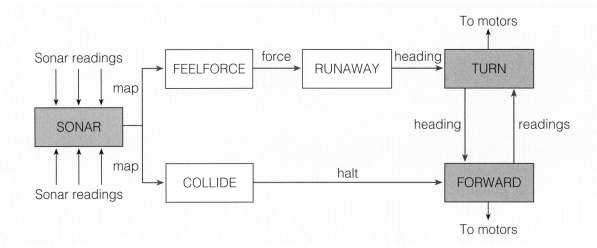

Figure 4.12   Subsumption architecture – Level 0

Briefly, the modules work together as follows:

▶ The SONAR module receives readings from all the sonar range detectors, filters out noise and then produces a map of the ranges to solid objects around the robot, which is then passed to the FEELFORCE and COLLIDE AFSMs.

▶ The COLLIDE module examines the map. If it finds an object straight ahead, it sends a 'halt' signal to the FORWARD module, causing the robot to stop.

▶ The FEELFORCE module treats each of the objects around the robot as a repulsive force, expressed as a vector. It adds all these vectors together, yielding a single new vector, which it passes to the RUNAWAY module.

Remember that a vector is a set of quantities. A force vector consists of two values: a magnitude and a direction.

▶ The RUNAWAY module inspects the force vector it has been sent and, when necessary, calculates an angle of turn, which it sends to the TURN AFSM connected to the robot's steering actuators.

The resulting behaviour can be quite complex. The robot will sit still until it is approached by a moving object on a collision course, whereupon it will turn 180° away from the object and move in this new direction. If another obstacle is ahead at this point the robot will stop, turn to such an angle as to avoid a new collision and move off in this direction.

We can now get an idea of how subsumption works by considering the Level 1 architecture of the same robot. Recall that the purpose of Level 1 is to give the robot wandering behaviour. Brooks's solution was to add just two new modules, WANDER and AVOID:

▶ The WANDER module generates a new random heading for the robot every few seconds. Since this cannot be passed directly to the TURN and FORWARD modules, as this would bypass the carefully contrived behaviour of Level 0, instead the heading vector is passed to the

▶ AVOID module, which computes a new heading by combining the heading it has received from WANDER with the force vector supplied by the FEELFORCE module in Level 0.

The new heading subsumes the heading calculated by the RUNAWAY module in Level 0, by suppressing the output of that module.

SAQ 4.7

What does suppression mean in the context of the subsumption architecture?

ANSWER...

The output of the subsuming module completely replaces the output of the lower-level one. The lower-level output stream is swapped for that of the higher-level one.

The combination of the two levels is shown in Figure 4.13.

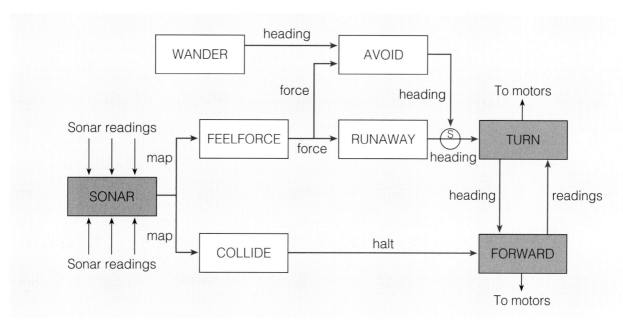

Figure 4.13   Subsumption architecture – Level 1

The result will be that the robot will wander at random until it encounters an obstacle. It will then modify its wandering behaviour to avoid the obstacle. Notice that nothing in Level 0 has been modified or replaced. New behaviour has simply been built on top of the earlier, more 'primitive', features. More sophisticated behaviour emerges from the interaction between the two levels.

Brooks added several other layers to the architecture. The third layer (Level 2) was concerned with the robot exploring its territory, finding places to visit and moving along corridors. The new layer consisted of six new AFSMs:

▶ STATUS monitors the activity of the TURN and FORWARD modules, sending out a binary busy/idle signal, as appropriate.

▶ WHENLOOK. If this module detects that the robot has been sitting idle for a certain length of time, it temporarily inhibits wandering, gathers some pictures of the immediate environment, and then moves the robot off in search of new horizons.

▶ LOOK takes pictures using an onboard camera and selects a suitable candidate space towards which to move.

▶ CORRIDOR uses the array of sonar detectors to locate corridors.

▶ INTEGRATE puts together the results of the robot's most recent movements and feeds these to:

▶ PATHPLAN combines the information it gets from LOOK and INTEGRATE to work out a path (an angle to turn and a distance to travel), which is then passed to the AVOID module.

Note then, that the subsumption of Level 1 by Level 2 works through the higher layer inhibiting the output of WANDER and suppressing the input of AVOID. The complete picture is given in Figure 4.14.

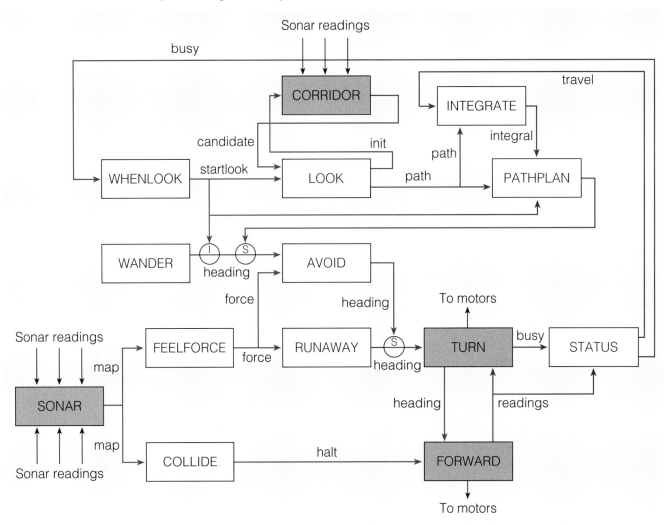

Figure 4.14   Subsumption architecture – Levels, 0, 1 and 2

You can see that it would be possible to add further layers without difficulty.

SAQ 4.8

Make a list of what you think are the main features of subsumption architectures.

ANSWER...

I came up with the following points:

▶ Behaviour is arranged in layers.

▶ Each layer is composed of a number of simple modules, signalling to one another across narrowband communication lines.

▶ Every module in every layer potentially has access to the same sensor information.

▶ A higher layer may subsume a lower one (but not the other way round) by either inhibiting or suppressing signals along the communication lines within the lower layer.

▶ Behaviour emerges from the interaction between modules within, and between, layers.

Subsumption architectures have been phenomenally popular in recent robotic research and development, particularly in the area of walking robots. Many very complex and successful exploration robot prototypes have been built using this approach. However, it's a good idea to try to think a bit critically about what you now know of subsumption architectures.

Exercise 4.2

Can you think of any possible drawbacks to the subsumption approach?

Discussion ....

I thought there might be a few possible problems.

▶ Firstly, there is the question of the adaptability of a subsumption system. Brooks and his colleagues worked very hard on the precise tuning of the internal modules and the connections between them. However, once these behaviours are incorporated into the machine, they can only be changed by reprogramming. The robot has no means of adapting in the light of experience.

▶ Programming a subsumption architecture is very difficult and involves a lot of trial and error.

▶ Once created, subsumption systems are hard to analyse and even harder to change.

▶ It is not clear how well a subsumption system will scale to produce more sophisticated behaviour. Adding more and more layers and AFSMs radically increases the programming difficulties.

The underlying principles and concepts of subsumption have been much adapted and modified since Brooks's pioneering work. Brooks himself specified a Behaviour Language, designed for writing large collections of subsumption architecture AFSMs. Other new ideas have included monostables (variables which are active for a specified time period) and registers (variables which can hold a range of values). Using these new ideas, machines of great complexity have been built. A good example is Hannibal, a hexapodal robot with over 100 sensors and 1500 AFSMs grouped into several dozen layers running on eight onboard computers.

Potential fields methods

You may or may not recall a small point I made among the detail of the descriptions above. In Level 0 of the subsumption architecture, I referred to a module FEELFORCE, whose task is to interpret surrounding objects as repulsive vectors and calculate a new vector to be used by the RUNAWAY module. RUNAWAY's function is to calculate an angle through which the robot should turn to avoid these obstacles. Perhaps this sounded slightly obscure to you at the time, although you may well have detected echoes of the cockroach and honeybee case studies of Unit 2. In fact, an entire approach to reactive robotics can be built on the idea of attractive and repulsive vectors: the *potential fields methods*.

Exercise 4.3 (optional)

There is a fair bit of discussion of vectors and their manipulation in this section, so if you feel you need some help, you may wish to look at the relevant sections in the section in the Maths Guide for this unit now.

We can start our discussion of potential fields (PF) strategies by considering the situation depicted in Figure 4.15. A robot is moving towards some goal, perhaps a source of 'food' or energy, but an obstacle lies in its path. As the robot makes its way towards the source, it will need to plot a course that skirts round the obstacle, but keeps it moving in the general direction of the goal.

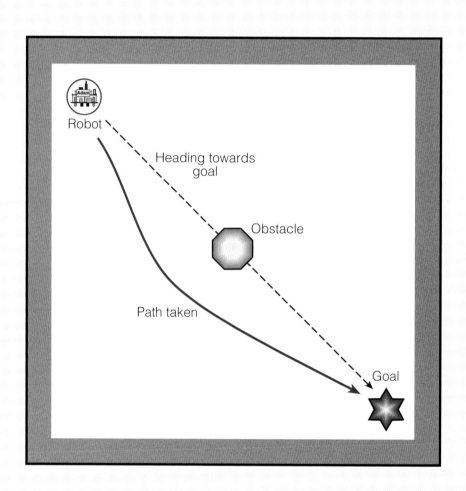

Figure 4.15   Robot obstructed as it moves towards a goal

One way of picturing the robot's situation is to think of the objects within its range as being surrounded by *fields* that will exert forces on it: the energy source will exercise an attractive force on the robot, the obstacle a repulsive one (see Figure 4.16). The field of force associated with each object is represented as an array of *force vectors*. Recall that a vector is a **tuple** of one or more quantities; each force vector is a 2-tuple (V_m, V_d), where V_m is the magnitude of the force and V_d its direction. In Figure 4.16, each vector is represented as an arrow, with the length of the arrow representing the quantity V_m and the direction of the arrow, naturally, representing V_d. Only some of the vectors are shown in the figure, but you should think of every point in the space around the objects as being occupied by a vector, thus making up a continuous field.

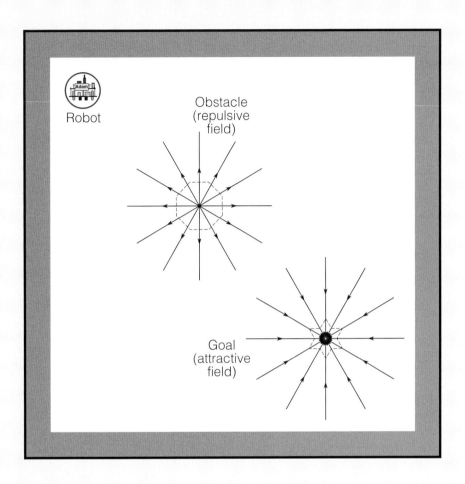

Figure 4.16   Objects with attractive and repulsive fields

Another, equivalent, way of depicting this world is to visualise it as a *landscape*, and the robot as a spherical object, such as a ball bearing, within it, as illustrated in Figure 4.17. The repulsive fields will be represented as hills, so the tendency of the robot will be to roll away from these; the attractive objects will lie at the bottom of valleys, with the robot naturally rolling towards them. For the rest of this discussion, however, I'll largely stick with the field and vector picture.

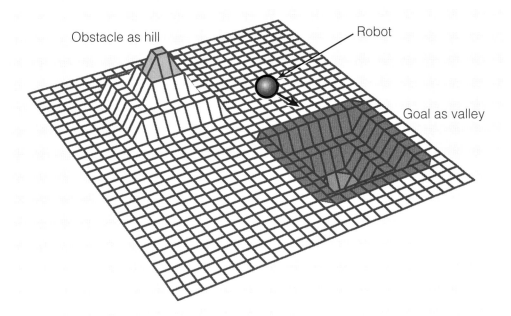

Figure 4.17   Objects creating hills and valleys in a potential field landscape

Look again at Figure 4.16. As I've already said, each vector represents the attractive or repulsive force exerted by objects in the space, with a vector at every point in it. But another way of interpreting a vector is as the *behaviour* that the robot should display when it is at that point. The vector specifies a magnitude and a direction: a robot that finds itself at the base of the vector's arrow should move in the direction *d* the arrow is pointing, with a speed proportional to *m*, the vector's magnitude. In the case of the obstacle illustrated in Figure 4.16, this will be given by:

$$\mathbf{V} = \begin{bmatrix} V_d = -\theta \\ V_m = c \end{bmatrix}$$

(4.1)

where θ is the angle at which the robot should move (negative because it should move *away* from the object) and *c* the velocity it should move at. Here the speed is a constant, no matter what distance the robot is from the object.

This raises quite a serious question. At what point does the attractive or repulsive influence of an object end? Clearly a robot situated a thousand metres from an object shouldn't be affected by it. At what point should its influence become felt? The simplest solution would be to draw an arbitrary boundary around the object and lay down that a robot situated anywhere within this boundary will feel a constant repulsive or attractive force, and anywhere outside it no force at all. There are dangers in this strategy, though. Think about this question for a moment.

Exercise 4.4

What might be the result of this scheme of arbitrary cut-off for a robot heading towards a goal and encountering the edge of an obstacle's repulsive field?

Discussion ....

The robot will be heading along a vector pointing towards its goal. At the moment it hits the edge of the obstacle's field it will turn and move away from the object along a new vector. This will immediately take it out of the obstacle's influence, whereupon it will naturally return to the vector taking it towards its goal. This, in turn, will bring the robot straight back into the repulsive field, which it will again back out of. The result will be an inefficient, jerky, bouncing movement around the edge of the obstacle's sphere of influence.

There are a number of strategies for avoiding this sort of inefficient behaviour. Fields can be arranged so that their influence falls off smoothly with increasing distance from the object at the centre. The rate at which the influence dies away can be either linear or exponential. For a linear drop-off the force is given by:

$$V_m = -xd + y \qquad (4.2)$$

For an exponential drop-off, the equation is:

$$V_m = -xd^2 + y \qquad (4.3)$$

strictly, this is a quadratic where d is the distance from the centre of the field, x is the rate of fall-off and y is a constant.

Returning to our earlier landscape picture of the fields, these three main types of field boundary are represented in Figures 4.18 (a) to (c).

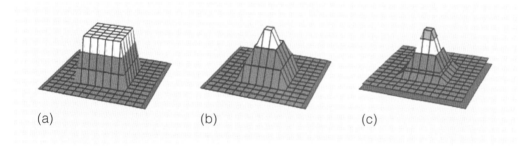

(a) (b) (c)

Figure 4.18   Three main types of field boundary: (a) Border cut-off. (b) Linear cut-off. (c) Exponential cut-off

Now consider a robot that has approached an obstacle with the repulsive field illustrated in Figure 4.19. Its distance detectors (sonar or infrared) discover an obstacle at distance d. The vector **V** along which the robot should now head is given by:

$$\mathbf{V} = \begin{bmatrix} V_d = -\theta \\ V_m = \begin{cases} \dfrac{D-d}{D} & \text{for } d \le D \\ 0 & \text{for } d > D \end{cases} \end{bmatrix} \qquad (4.4)$$

where D is some limit, fixed by the designer, on how near an object must be before it can influence the robot.

This is simple enough, as we're dealing with only a single object. But what will happen when there are a number of objects in the robot's vicinity, all exerting an influence on it? The answer is fairly clear: the robot has to *combine* the fields in some way. This is simple to do; at every update point, the robot just *sums* all of the vectors that are acting on it and heads off along the **resultant**, the vector that results from this calculation.

As a simple example, examine the situation of the robot in Figure 4.19. The machine is moving along a vector that is attracting it towards the goal. However, at the point indicated in the figure, it updates its sensors and detects a repulsive field emanating from the obstacle. How should it respond? The obvious response is to find a compromise between the two forces acting on it. It achieves this simply by *adding* the two vectors and moving on a heading indicated by the resultant vector's direction and at a speed given in the resultant vector's magnitude. The resultant is shown in Figure 4.19.

Remember that the direction of the vector is represented by the direction of the arrow and the magnitude by the length of the arrow.

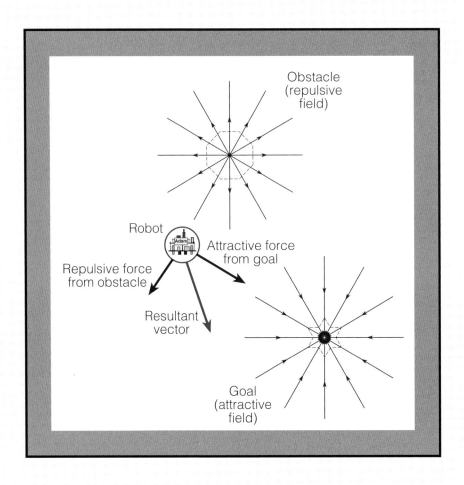

Figure 4.19   Robot updates its heading vector under the influence of two fields

Just to reinforce the idea, try this exercise.

Exercise 4.5

A robot is travelling on a heading of 45° at a speed of 8.5 cm s^{-1} (centimetres per second), when its sensors detect a force from a nearby obstacle impelling it to move away at a heading of 333.4° at 4.5 cm s^{-1}. What will be its new direction and speed? If you're uncertain about adding vectors, refer to the Maths Guide for the course or use a vector calculator.

Discussion ....

We can picture the robot's situation as in Figure 4.20. Drawing in its resultant vector, we can calculate using basic trigonometry that the magnitude (the length of the arrow) of the resultant is 10.8 and its direction 21.8°. The robot will therefore start to move at 10.8 cm s^{-1} on a heading of 21.8°.

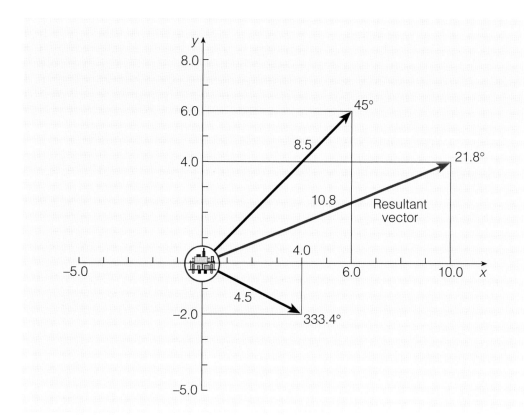

Figure 4.20   Vectors acting on a robot and their resultant

Another way of visualising this is to imagine the entire space as filled with vector arrows, one at every point, each representing the resultant force from the field at that point. But this is a bit misleading. The fields have no real existence. They are just the set of vectors that the robot would calculate from its sensor readings and then combine.

Potential fields can be of many types and can be combined to work on robots in interesting ways. To take one example, consider the sort of corridor-following behaviour that you encountered when we discussed subsumption architectures. Ideally, the robot will move smoothly down the corridor, preferably on a straight line down the middle, but certainly avoiding collision with the walls (see Figure 4.21(a)). How could this be managed using the potential fields approach?

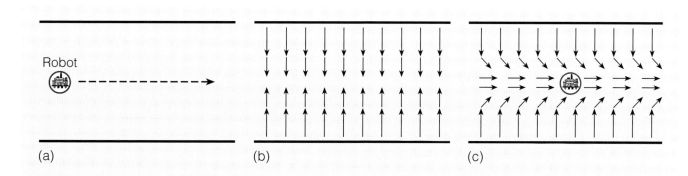

(a)   (b)   (c)

Figure 4.21   Robot moving along a corridor. (a) Ideal robot path (b) Perpendicular field. (c) Resultant field

SAQ 4.9

How do you think this could be managed using the PF approach?

ANSWER...

Given that the imperative is not to hit the walls, a uniform repulsive field emanating from them seems like a good start.

We can set this up easily enough: such a field is illustrated in Figure 4.21(b). Note that it is of rather a different shape from the kind we have illustrated so far. The force vectors point out perpendicularly from along the walls, and diminish in magnitude linearly with distance. For obvious reasons, this kind of field is known as **perpendicular**.

Fairly clearly, though, this wouldn't be enough in itself. A robot inside such a field would certainly not hit the walls, as it would feel a constant force vector pushing it away from them. However, there is no reason at all why it should move along the corridor – so we have to add a second field whose vectors point along the middle of the corridor. The combined effect of the two fields is illustrated in Figure 4.21(c).

The combined result of the two fields should be for the robot to move smoothly along the corridor, keeping the two walls equidistant from it.

Now let's make the problem a little more difficult by placing an obstacle somewhere in the corridor, quite near to one of the walls. In practice, the robot could go either way round the object, but the path between it and the nearest wall is not the best choice – too much chance of a collision. The ideal path is to take the solid one marked in Figure 4.22 (a). How can this be achieved with a field? Well, obviously the obstacle needs a repulsive field of some kind. However, the type we've shown in Figure 4.22(b), the kind of radial, repulsive field we've been working with up to now, may not be the best possibility. There are two reasons for this:

1   It's quite possible that the repulsive vectors on the wall side of the object might push the robot straight into the wall.

2   Worse, there is also a distinct possibility that the robot, moving forward on a vector to take it down the corridor, might meet a vector of equal magnitude pointing in exactly the opposite direction. The overall effect would be that the two vectors would cancel each other out and the robot would sit, going nowhere, caught between two equal and opposite forces. This is yet another example of a local minimum problem: there are points on the landscape where the field has zero strength.

Figure 4.22(c) indicates one way out of the problem. Instead of the usual radial field, the obstacle has been given a **tangential** field. The arrows of force flow around the object, at a tangent to it, their general direction indicating the preferred way round.

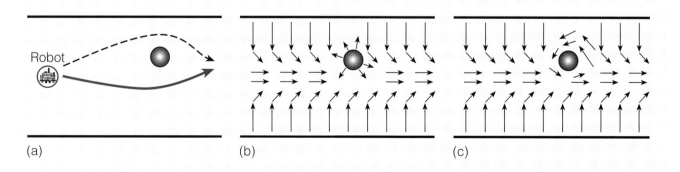

(a)   (b)   (c)

Figure 4.22   Obstacle placed in the corridor: (a) Possible paths. (b) Radial field from obstacle. (c) Tangential field

Now is the time to sum up what you've learned about the potential fields strategy.

SAQ 4.10

Sum up what you think are the main points of the PF approach. What similarities and differences can you see between potential fields strategies and subsumption architectures?

ANSWER...

I thought that the approach has the following main features:

▶ In PF, the robot perceives the world in terms of attractive and repulsive fields, of various shapes and configurations; in this way, objects exist for the robot as affordances.

▶ Robots respond to these fields by vector summation.

▶ Complex behaviour can emerge from combining potential fields from several objects.

Among the similarities and differences with subsumption architectures, I found these:

▶ Like subsumption architectures, the potential fields (PF) approach is another behaviour-based approach to robotics. Behaviours link perception (sensing a field and summing vectors) directly to action (motor commands resulting from the summed vectors).

▶ In PF, unlike subsumption architectures, there is no explicit layering of behaviour.

It's quite possible you thought of others.

Finally, and just to return for a moment to the main themes of the course, potential fields systems are another example of *emergence*. Complex, seemingly purposeful behaviour emerges from interactions. In subsumption architectures, the interaction is mainly between internal components. Although PF robots are also likely to have some degree of internal interaction, the whole approach seems to be much more closely modelled on the behaviour you read about in the honeybee and cockroach studies in Unit 2. You'll recall that in these cases, the behaviour emerged from a close coupling of the creature with key features of its environment, with only quite minimal internal processing taking place. Have a quick look back at Case Studies 2.2 and 2.3 if you've forgotten any of this.

Other approaches

In Unit 2, we looked at the question of insect walking. Far from being a straightforward mechanical process, beneath the notice of artificial intelligence, it turned out that insect walking is an intricate and ill-understood behaviour arising from complex internal interactions within the insect. I offered a brief summary of the theory of these interactive mechanisms.

Can some of this theory be applied to robotic research? Could some of the limitations you saw in Ambler be thereby overcome?

Case Study 4.4: Insect-walking robots

In a series of experiments conducted between 1991 and 1997, roboticists Roger Quinn, Hillel Chiel and Roy Ritzmann developed a number of robotic models of hexapodal walking, inspired by the known facts of locomotion in actual insects, such as cockroaches and stick insects. The earliest and most straightforward of these models, although a considerable simplification of the biological reality, relies on intricate interactions. I'll take it a step at a time.

As you learned in Unit 2, in real insects there is no evidence of any central controller, as one would find in a conventional robot. Instead, control of each leg seems to rest with the leg itself. In Beer et al.'s (1997) model, then, the movements of each leg are handled by a separate module, with each module comprising several units (see Figure 4.23). These units signal to one another with one of two possible messages: an **excitatory** signal, which encourages the unit being signalled to start working or work harder; and an **inhibitory** signal, which does the reverse – it slows down the work of the unit signalled to or stops it working altogether. Excitatory or inhibitory signals can be of varying strengths. These two types of connection are represented in Figure 4.23 by contrasting line styles. The mechanics of a stride are as follows:

1   A pacemaker unit (P) sends out periodic bursts of signals to the forward swing actuator (FS), which starts it moving the leg forward, and inhibitory ones to the backward swing actuator (BS), shutting down any possible backward movement.

2   The leg lifts and swings forward to its furthest forward position.

3   A sensory unit (FAS) starts sending signals when it detects that the leg has reached its extreme forward position. It sends an excitatory message to the foot control actuator (FT), which plants the foot firmly on the ground, and to the backward swing actuator, which then begins the backward movement of the leg.

4   At the same time, FAS sends inhibitory messages to FS and to P, effectively shutting them down, so that nothing will interfere with the backward push.

5   Another sensory unit (BAS) detects when the leg has reached its extreme backward position and sends an excitatory signal to P, allowing it to start the cycle again.

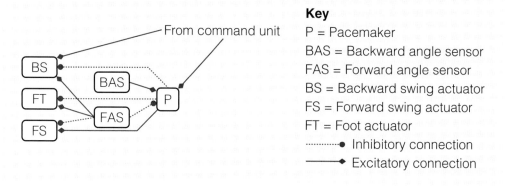

Key
P = Pacemaker
BAS = Backward angle sensor
FAS = Forward angle sensor
BS = Backward swing actuator
FS = Forward swing actuator
FT = Foot actuator
............• Inhibitory connection
————► Excitatory connection

Figure 4.23   Single leg controller

A single command unit sends identical excitatory signals to the P and BS units of all the leg control modules. However, the command unit has no overall controlling function: it simply provides the impetus for the insect to start moving in the first place. There is no central control of the stride: the work is shared or **distributed** among a number of units and the interactions between them. But how are the various legs coordinated to give the characteristic gaits we looked at above? Isn't a central regulator necessary there? If we take a closer look at Beer et al.'s model, we can see that it isn't. The coordination is achieved in two ways:

▶   The pacemaker units of adjacent leg control modules are simply connected together, and send inhibitory messages to one another. This stops adjacent legs from making a step at the same time: while one leg is swinging forward, the next leg along will remain in the stance position. Beer discovered that this mechanism alone can produce the tripodal gait illustrated in Unit 2, Figure 2.6.

▶   The period between bursts of signals in the pacemaker units of the back legs are tuned to be slightly slower than those of the legs further forwards. This produces the typical metachronal wave at lower speeds.

The entire model is presented in Figure 4.24. It was found to be capable of reproducing any of the typical insect walking patterns and also to be extremely resilient to damage. With single sensors removed and some connections deleted, the robot was still capable of efficient movement.

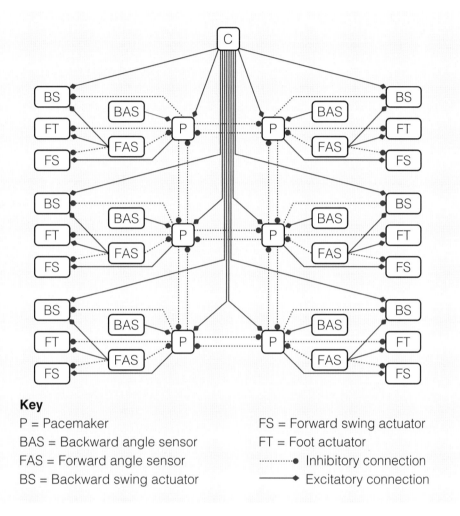

Key

P = Pacemaker

BAS = Backward angle sensor

FAS = Forward angle sensor

BS = Backward swing actuator

FS = Forward swing actuator

FT = Foot actuator

·········• Inhibitory connection

————➤ Excitatory connection

Figure 4.24   Complete walking architecture

The group experimented with a number of other control mechanisms, all sharing the kind of distributed, interactive pattern of the first. These mechanisms were tested out in a real robot (Robot 1, Figure 4.25(a)). A glance at the picture will show you how basic this early model was. Although the robot reproduced the full range of gaits observed in insects, and could change smoothly between them as it moved at different speeds, it could still only cope with level surfaces.

(a)

(b)

Figure 4.25   (a) Robot I. (b) Robot 2

Real insects use multi-jointed legs to negotiate slippery, sloping, obstacle-strewn terrain with ease. In 1994, Beer and his colleagues developed a much more sophisticated robot (Robot 2 in Figure 4.25(b)), each leg of which had four joints, all connected in a highly distributed control system similar to that of Robot 1. This robot was able to handle much more complicated surfaces by means of a number of additional strategies, including:

▶ *active and passive compliance*: this enabled the robot to maintain balance on rough ground by altering the position and stiffness of its leg joints, and distributing body weight evenly over the standing legs;

▶ *stepping reflex*: as the robot's leg moved from swing into stance position, it was moved into a position where it would give maximum stability;

▶ *elevator reflex*: when a swinging leg met an obstruction, it was lifted upwards and over it;

▶ *search reflex*: if a swinging leg was unable to find a secure footing, it searched around and ahead of its original intended foothold for a suitable place to plant the leg.

To repeat: none of these reflexes was centrally controlled. As in the case of Robot 1, individual units were responsible for each joint, spring and sensor. The robot's entire repertoire of walking behaviours arose from the interactions between them.

As Beer et al. (1997) point out, their second model is still a gross simplification of the natural reality. Insects are immensely capable walkers. Their muscles are, weight for weight, extremely powerful; their legs have many degrees of freedom, and are equipped with flexible segments and specialised claws for gripping. Insect legs also have hundreds of sensors that supply information about the limb's movements and position. An insect's antennae also supply a wealth of sensory feedback relevant to walking, all of which is somehow integrated into the whole. As I've said before, our 'simple' insect is very far from simple.

Let's now recap one point that will be of importance later.

SAQ 4.11

Using your own words, jot down what you think are *excitatory* and *inhibitory* signals. What do you think would happen if a module received an excitatory and an inhibitory signal simultaneously?

ANSWER..

Excitatory signals are messages to some unit that prompt it to start working, make it more likely to start working, or make it work harder if it is working already; inhibitory signals prompt a unit to stop working, or make it less likely to start working, or make it work less hard. If an excitatory and inhibitory signal arrived at the same time, they would tend to cancel each other out, so that – if they were of equal strength – they would have no effect on the module at all.

To sum up this long section: sophisticated behaviour – purposive movement and obstacle avoidance – can arise without explicit thought and reasoning through a close coupling of sensors, actuators and environment.

And finally, to reinforce your understanding of reactive robotics generally, try the following computer exercise.

Computer Exercise 4.1

Load Computer Exercise 4.1 on the DVD and follow the instructions.

3 Adaptation and selection

In Unit 2, I identified two forms of adaptation. As a quick test of memory try the following question.

SAQ 4.12

What were the two forms of adaptation we distinguished in Unit 2?

ANSWER..

Adaptation that takes place during the lifetime of the individual; and adaptation of a species over many generations.

At the time, I kept these two kinds of adaptation strictly apart, reserving the use of the term *adaptation* just for the first of them. I also singled out *learning* as one of the most important kinds of adaptive change. Without learning, a system has little claim to be called intelligent. However, the truth is that in the fields of machine learning and adaptive, behaviour-based robotics, the distinction between adaptive change and evolutionary change becomes – as you will see – very blurred. To create adaptive, learning systems, researchers are just as likely to use techniques based on the principles of Darwinian selection as ideas from conventional theories of learning.

The quantity and scope of the research in these fields is vast. I can do no more than just skim the surface here. So in this section I want to consider just three broad questions: if adaptation means learning or change of some kind, then:

▶ what kinds of things can be learned?

▶ how is learning brought about?

▶ what adaptations happen inside a system that account for learning?

The real problem here is that there is no comprehensive theory of learning, and no real agreement about what can be learned or how learning takes place. All we have at this stage is a bewildering variety of theories, strategies and techniques. So the best I can do is to offer some fairly general answers to these three questions, illustrating them with a few significant examples. I'm going to base this discussion mainly on the examples of Toto and Beer et al.'s walking insects, as well as the following case study.

Case Study 4.5: Adam

This is a slightly simplified account of experiments carried out by Andrew Russell (2004) at Monash University.

Adam (ADAptive Mobile robot) is a small wheeled robot that inhabits an artificial world called EDEN (EDucational ENvironment), consisting of a square enclosure about 1.5 × 1.5 metres (see Figure 4.26) surrounded by a wall. In moving around EDEN, Adam expends energy, which it needs to renew whenever it can. While moving, it uses a certain amount of energy; while stationary (basking) it only uses half as much. Collisions with the wall also mean a drain on Adam's energy.

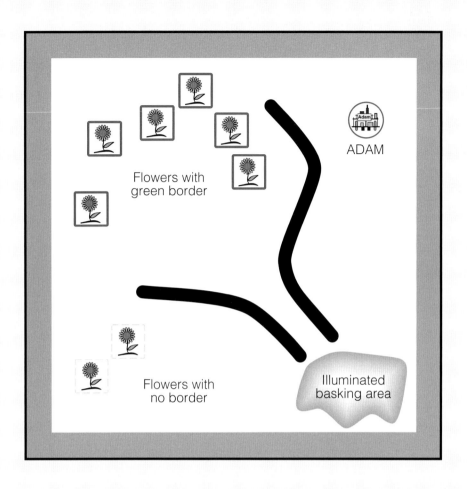

Figure 4.26   EDEN

Adam is able to gather information about its environment through a number of sensors, including front-mounted collision sensors, light sensors and sound sensors. It also has colour sensors mounted on its base, allowing the robot to perceive the colour of the area of floor under it. The 'flowers' depicted in Figure 4.26 are aluminium plates on the floor, through which Adam can draw energy through a retractable proboscis.

Some of these flowers are surrounded by a green border that can be sensed by the robot; others have no border and are thus effectively invisible to it. Without going into any detail at this stage, Adam's internal structure is reactive, comprising a number of interacting *behaviours*, which handle its responses to light, collision, and so on. Adam is endowed with a certain amount of learning power. It stores memories of what has happened to it in the past, specifically sequences of sensor readings that led to a response from its actuators – for instance, sensing the red boundary before the wall and then the subsequent collision, which led to its motors backing away from the wall. From these memories, Adam is able to form associations between past events and learn reflexive responses to them. For example, Adam can learn to:

▶ associate floor colour with imminent collisions. The robot starts backing up as soon as it senses the red boundary area, thus avoiding a collision with the wall that would drain its energy;

▶ associate noises with the ability to feed from the invisible flowers. Experimenters trained Adam by smacking two pieces of wood together as it was feeding. Thereafter, as Adam approached any of the invisible flowers, this sound cue caused it to start feeding, even though it couldn't sense the flower was there.

Figure 4.27   Adam 'basking'

These look rather like conditioned reflexes. Russell was also able to demonstrate that Adam could undergo operant conditioning by teaching it to turn left towards the flowers when it encountered one of the thick black lines.

3.1 What is learned?

So what, in general terms, does Adam learn? The obvious answer is to associate certain sensor readings with certain external events – for example, it came to relate the red line just inside EDEN's boundary with an imminent collision, or a green colour detected by its floor sensors with feeding. These learned reactions allowed it to anticipate both harmful and beneficial events, and thus to conserve its energy reserves. There are plenty of other examples of the kinds of things that researchers have persuaded robots, and computer systems more generally, to learn. These include:

▶ recognising patterns;

▶ devising strategies;

▶ predicting environmental changes;

▶ recognising and responding to the strategies of other robots;

▶ generating complete new sets of behaviours or internal modules;

▶ exchanging information with other robots.

Clearly, the range of possibilities is huge, and the range of strategies that researchers have used to bring about these results is similarly wide and diverse. In the next two subsections let's look briefly at these.

3.2 How is learning brought about?

Learning in an artificial system implies a learning regime. There must be some form of *process* through and within which adaptation or learning can take place. Such processes may be roughly classified under the following broad headings:

▶ supervised learning
▶ reinforcement learning
▶ learning by imitation
▶ learning by evolution.

Of course, with such a vast research area as machine learning other classifications are possible. However, this will serve our purposes as a rough guide.

Supervised learning

Supervised learning presupposes a bank of *training data*, usually a set of exemplars. Each exemplar will be a *pair*, consisting of:

▶ an input object: generally this will be a vector containing a number of features that define the object;
▶ a 'correct' or desired output object: what this will be depends on what it is we want the system to learn. One popular use of supervised learning is to teach systems to classify their inputs. In the case of a system like this, the output object will be the label of the class the input object should be put in.

The system is required to learn from the training set a *function* that will accurately map *any* input object onto the correct output object. You will see a great many examples of this kind of learning regime in Block 4.

Reinforcement learning

In Unit 2, I briefly mentioned theories of animal (and human) learning that arise from behaviourism. You may remember that these theories embody the idea of *conditioning*, the learned association of some stimulus with a response. The most influential form of these has been *operant conditioning*, where particular actions are rewarded, and so reinforced. Reinforcement learning has been used in a wide variety of computer learning systems, but it is probably simplest to think about it in terms of its application in robotics.

Reinforcement learning is unsupervised: there is no external teacher with omniscient access to the correct answer at every step. Instead, the system learns by selecting actions and then receiving punishments or rewards in return. In the case of Adam exploring its environment, obviously these punishments and rewards come from the environment itself – finding an energy source is rewarding, for example; colliding with a wall, a punishment. Reinforcement learning systems learn through their mistakes and their successes.

We can state this rather more formally as follows. For an agent exploring an environment, there will be:

▶ a set of possible environmental states S;
▶ an input function I, which determines how the robot perceives each environmental state;
▶ a set of actions A at the agent's disposal;
▶ a set of possible reinforcement signals, usually $\{0, 1\}$.

The agent's task is to learn a policy P, such that for every environmental state in S, an action is selected from A which is the optimal choice. This is easy enough if one only has to consider the immediate reward – all the agent has to do is learn which actions give the best reward in every state. However, the best rewards may not be the most immediate; and immediate rewards may well lead to longer-term disaster. This is because performing an action from A will put the agent in a new state, in which a new set of actions is available, all of which could lead to poor results. For example, a robot's choice to move in a certain direction may lead it straight to an energy source. However, the source may be situated at the edge of a cliff, with nowhere to go thereafter but down.

There a number of well-known algorithms for reinforcement learning, the most successful of which are **adaptive heuristic critic** and **Q-learning**. To describe these in detail would take us beyond the scope of this course. I've provided links and some further commentary on the course DVD.

Clearly, reinforcement learning is an ideal approach for autonomous systems: no teacher with perfect knowledge of how a task should be accomplished is necessary. Reinforcement learning simply finds a mapping from perceptual states to actions that maximises long-term reward. However, designing and programming the reward system can prove very difficult. A robot that can guide its own learning process – that can learn how best to learn, termed **metalearning** – is a long-term ideal for reinforcement learning systems.

Learning by imitation

Many roboticists are now experimenting in a new field, known as **social robotics** or **human–robot interaction**. As its name suggests, the goal of this work is to develop robots that, in the words of Cynthia Breazeal of the Robotic Life Laboratory at MIT, are 'capable of cooperating with us as capable partners'. She goes on:

> For me, the ultimate vision of a socially intelligent robot is one that is able to communicate and interact with us, understand and even relate to us, in a personal way.

Source: Breazeal (2005), p. 19

Examples of recently developed robots, or systems under development, with the beginnings of this sort of social intelligence are:

- ▶ robotic pets, such as Sony's dog *Aibo*;
- ▶ healthcare assistants, including robotic walkers that escort patients to appointments;
- ▶ robotic tutors and companions in childcare;
- ▶ automated, socially capable tour guides and museum attendants;
- ▶ robotic astronauts, such as NASA's *Robonaut*.

It seems obvious that some of the interactions that future robots might have with humans would be in the realm of learning. Robots that can learn, rather than being hard-coded for specific purposes, will have obvious advantages: they can readily adapt to new tasks, saving immense amounts of specialised programming effort. There has been successful research into teaching robots through gestures and natural language. However, *imitation* also looks like a promising direction.

There can be no question that much human learning, particularly in our earliest years, arises from imitation of the old by the young. Mothers and babies play imitation games like 'pat-a-cake' together. You've already seen, in Units 1 and 2, examples of animals that learn new skills from their parents. In the absence of any possible linguistic communication between such animals, such learned behaviour must come from imitation.

Case Study 4.6: Robots learning from humans

Maja Mataric has reported recent experiments in which a mobile robot learns to carry out tasks in which it is required to negotiate a cluttered environment of large coloured cylinders, picking up smaller coloured objects and depositing them at goal locations. An example of such a task is given in Figure 4.28. The tasks are made more difficult by blocking certain paths, making some objects inaccessible, or even specifying targets that don't exist (see Figure 4.29).

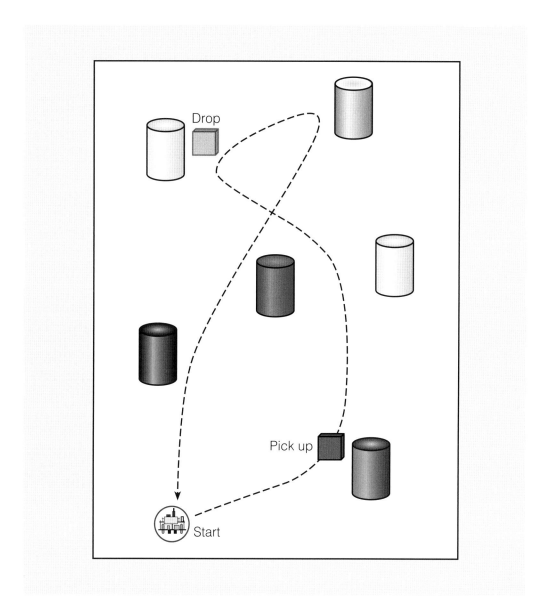

Figure 4.28 Robot task

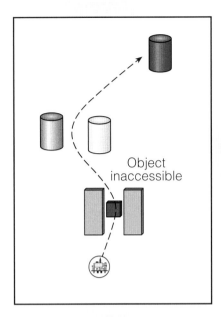 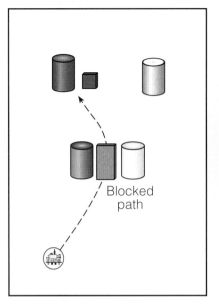 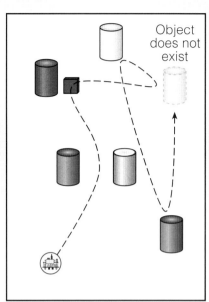

Figure 4.29   Robot may need to seek human help

The robot is expected to learn a task by having it demonstrated by a human, one or more times, and actively taking part in each demonstration, experiencing it through its own sensors. It then practices the task, receiving feedback from the human teacher. During the practice, it may seek help from the teacher or from any other human present (who may or may not be willing to help – the robot has to judge this for itself) if it gets stuck. It can signal its need for help in ways reminiscent of a pet dog – for example, by moving backwards and forwards between the teacher and the place where it is having problems, and by miming the action it wants to carry out (picking up a hard-to-reach object, say) with its actuators. Each of the teaching demonstrations may be slightly different, and may contain unnecessary steps, inconsistencies and other mistakes. The robot is expected to generalise the correct task from the demonstrations.

We will return to this work briefly in the next section. There have been considerable advances in human–robot communication of this type in recent years. Experimental systems now exist that are capable of playing games with humans, interpreting their intentions and goals and communicating their own, through a range of facial and bodily gestures and cues.

3.3 What adapts?

These, then, are some of the main strategies. But we've been missing something so far. The main point is this: adaptation must mean *change* of some kind. So what is *changing* inside a robot as it learns?

It would be pleasant if I could just give you the definitive answer and move on. But, as you probably guessed straight away, there is no such answer. Even in my short survey, you've already seen a whole range of systems and architectures – and of course there are plenty of other possibilities that I haven't had the space to cover. Since these systems have little or nothing in common, the ways in which they alter internally as a result of experience, are bound to have little in common as well. The best I can do is to look at some examples and try to make some generalisations.

Exercise 4.6

As a basis for the discussion of this section, think back to the following case studies:

1   Case Study 4.3 – Toto

2   Case Study 4.4 – Beer et al.'s walking robot

3   Case Study 4.5 – Adam.

All of these were capable of adaptive learning in one way or another. In general terms, what would need to change in each case for the learning to take place?

Discussion ....

In the absence of detailed knowledge of the internal structures of these systems, it's difficult to give anything but the most general answers. We'll consider the details shortly. At this point one might say this:

1   *Toto.* We know only that Toto builds maps and its internal structure is a subsumption architecture. The robot will require some sort of data structure in which to build the map, which must interface efficiently with the lower-level behaviour architecture.

2   *Walking robot.* This creature adapts its gait to different terrains, but this is not really a form of learning – it is a pre-programmed feature of the system. However, robots of this kind can adapt their gait in the event of damage, and this *is* a form of learning. Given the machine's uncluttered architecture of simple controllers connected by excitatory or inhibitory links, there are only two possibilities for change: either the behaviour of the controllers has to alter, or the links between them.

3   *Adam.* We've already noted that Adam learns associations between perceptual data recorded by its sensors (green patch, detected by floor sensor; collision, detected by crash sensors) with certain actions that it has to take in response (feed; stop and reverse). Essentially, Adam is learning a set of rules (IF green_patch THEN extend_proboscis, etc.). How precisely these rules are encoded in the system will depend on the system architecture.

This is obviously all rather general. Let's now look at some of these adaptive robots in a bit more detail.

Adam

Adam's internal, onboard architecture is very simple and purely reactive, as depicted in Figure 4.30. However, you'll notice the off-board PC, connected to Adam by an umbilical cable. This controls the learning system. The internal reactive system is encoded simply as a set of basic associations, or rules, for example:

IF left bumper activated THEN back off and turn clockwise
IF both floor colour sensors see green THEN feed and move forward

and so on. These are presumed to be 'primitive' behaviours that would have evolved in a real animal over millions of years. Many practical approaches to adaptation in robots and other AI systems begin in this way, with a certain level of basic behaviour which is then modified by experience. In Adam these basic behaviours are not encoded in the specific form we've given here, but are embedded in the structure of the microcontroller.

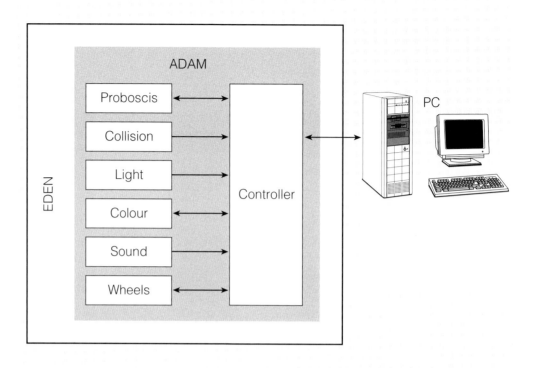

Figure 4.30   Adam's internal architecture

Learning takes place off-board. Any learning, however simple, entails a *memory* of some sort, however short term. In Adam's case, what is recorded is associations. The state R of the robot at any instant i is defined as:

$$R_i = (A_i, S_i) \tag{4.5}$$

where S_i is the state of the sensors at instant i and A_i is the state of the actuators at i. An event starting at instant j is defined as any change in the state of the robot:

$$(A_j - A_{j-1}) \cup (S_j - S_{j-1}) \neq \phi \tag{4.6}$$

(ϕ is the empty set). This change in state always begins with a change in sensor readings, since the robot is reactive. Simplifying slightly, the entire history of the robot, comprising all the events that have happened to it, is represented by M. The off-board computer records associations, where an association $\alpha(R_1)$ is the most frequently occurring set of events in M beginning with state R_1 and ending with a change in actuator state. Adam's regime is a clear example of reinforcement learning.

Having learned these associations, the off-board PC will override the behaviour of Adam's internal controller whenever it detects the last instant of an association, substituting the actuator change that it has recorded as taking place at the end of the association.

Toto

Toto learns maps. However, it's important to contrast these maps with the precise, hard-wired, whole-world structures of robots like Shakey and Ambler. Toto's job is to explore its environment and build up a rough map of its large-scale structure, sufficient for it to be able to negotiate it effectively.

For Toto, then, a map is an internal representation assembly of large-scale landmarks, such as walls, corridors, and so on. Since robotic sensors tend to be quite inaccurate, and give inconsistent readings, and since the environment may contain transitory objects, such as people moving around, the mechanism by means of which Toto detects and registers landmarks is designed to be very robust. It is based on rough sensor measurements and especially on the robot's own movements. For example, the presence of a wall would be suggested by a consistent compass bearing and unvarying sonar distance. Irregularities are averaged out and transient readings ignored. The recognition of a landmark is expressed with a certain degree of *confidence*, and when this confidence passes a threshold the landmark is acknowledged and recorded.

Toto stores its map as a linear list of nodes (see Figure 4.31). To be consistent with the robot's reactive subsumption architecture, each node is an AFSM, which receives inputs from the landmark detector AFSM and the sensors, and sends outputs to other nodes in the map. The map is initialised to a list of empty nodes; as Toto explores, sensor readings and landmark detection confidences are broadcast simultaneously to every node in the list. If no existing node matches these readings, then the next available empty node is set up for the new landmark, at the same time sending a *wake-up* signal to its neighbour. However, if the readings match a node already in the list, that node wakes up and sends an *expectation* signal to its next neighbour. Thus, Toto is ready to encounter the next landmark along the path before it comes within sensor range.

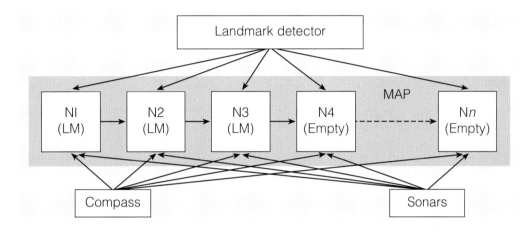

Figure 4.31   Toto internal map

Mataric's learning robot

This is a fairly standard reactive robot with the kind of internal architecture of interacting behaviours that you are now familiar with, in this case implemented in AYLLU, a special purpose robotic control system (Nicolescu and Mataric, 2005). Examples of the primitive behaviours from which complex task execution emerges would include `PickUp (Object-Colour)` or `Drop(Object)`. A complex task such as the one depicted in Figure 4.28 will therefore consist of a behaviour network of these simpler tasks, represented by a task network, as in Figure 4.32.

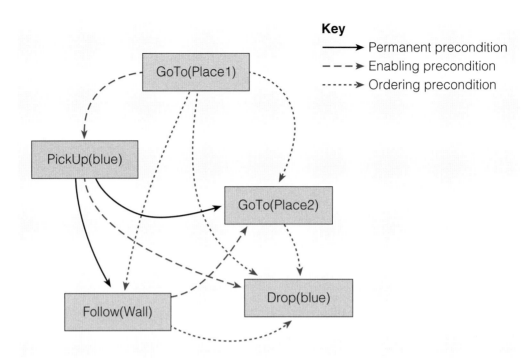

Figure 4.32   Task network

As I stated earlier, the robot is required to learn such networks, usually by generalising from a number of demonstrations, each of which may be faulty or inefficient in some way. We need not look at the details of the learning algorithm here.

Exercise 4.7

Obviously the adaptation taking place inside each of these three examples is quite different, reflecting their different internal designs. But do you think they have anything in common? Note down any rough ideas you have about this.

Discussion ....

Very generally, I thought that in all three cases:

▶ the learning component is something *added* to the reactive architecture, rather than an adaptation of the basic behavioural system itself;

▶ the purpose of this additional component is to retain a *memory* of events that had happened to the robot in the past;

▶ there is a basic, fixed level of reactive behaviour that the learning system *supplements*, or *overrides*, in some way. In biological terms, this is seen as equivalent to the behaviour acquired through evolution, and with which an animal is born.

The first point deserves a little more discussion. In all of the above cases, the underlying reactive architecture has remained unchanged, while new layers of software, capable of storing suitable representations or generalisations of past events, are built above it. This is in keeping with the principles of subsumption, but are there alternatives? Is there any way the primitive structures themselves can be modified to incorporate these memories? Let's think about Beer's walking robot for a moment.

Beer's walking robot

You'll remember that in this system sophisticated and robust walking behaviour emerges from the interactions of an assembly of interconnected leg controllers and pacemakers. The controllers themselves are very simple, each just responding straightforwardly to the *strength* of the signals it receives from the other controllers. You should recall, too, that I described the connections themselves as being either excitatory or inhibitory. This opens up an interesting possibility. If we make adjustments to the *strengths* of these connections, making them more or less excitatory, or more or less inhibitory, as a result of experience, this too should have an effect on the robot's subsequent behaviour. It would be another form of adaptation, of learning.

Hang on to this point. Adaptive behaviour can be brought about by modifying the strengths of the connections between interactive parts. We will leave the matter there for the moment; but most of your study in Block 4 will centre on exactly this idea.

3.4 Learning through evolution

Although it is not strictly the sort of adaptive alteration I identified in Unit 2, evolution itself can be thought of as a form of learning, in which whole species, over millions of years, 'learn' the body shapes and behaviours that will best fit them for their environments. I briefly outlined the remorseless process that appears to be the engine of this learning, Darwin's natural selection, in Unit 2. Modern researchers are happy to mimic the process on computers to find elegant adaptations of their systems.

Variations on this process, known broadly as a **genetic algorithm**, are very popular in the field of adaptive robotics and AI. We'll look briefly at an example in Case Study 4.7. The theory and practice of genetic algorithms, a major branch of a research endeavour known as **evolutionary computing**, we will cover in detail in Block 5.

Case Study 4.7: Sorting algorithms

One of the classic problems of computer science is the problem of *sorting*. To assemble a list of comparable elements – for example, e, g, c, b – into its alphabetically sorted form – b, c, e, g – may seem a pretty trivial exercise, but given that we may be dealing with arrays that are possibly millions of elements long, to be sorted in real time, the need for the most efficient sorting procedures possible is acute. All sorting algorithms involve a series of *comparisons* and *exchanges* between items in the input list. Here is an example: to sort the list e, g, c, b, first let's number each of the elements, as follows:

1	2	3	4
e	g	c	b

Now we can adopt the following sorting procedure:

1 Compare element 1 with element 3. Since e > c, swap them, giving:

1	2	3	4
c	g	e	b

2   Compare element 2 with element 4. Since g > b, swap them, giving:

3   Compare element 1 with element 4. Since c < g, there is no need for a swap.
4   Compare element 2 with element 3. Since b < e, there is no need for a swap.
5   Compare element 1 with element 2. Since c > b, swap them giving:

6   Compare element 3 with element 4. Since e < g, there is no need for a swap.
7   The array is now sorted, as no further swaps are possible.

So a *sorting procedure* boils down to an *order* in which pairs of elements can be compared and swapped. In our example above, the order was [(1,3), (2,4), (1,4), (2,3), (1,2)]. Such procedures are sometimes called **sorting networks**. Obviously for, say, a 16-element list, there is a very large number of possible sorting networks, some of which will be very efficient, others much less so. Sorting networks can be represented quite neatly in pictorial form, as in this example.

Figure 4.33 illustrates a sorting procedure known as a Batcher sort, working on the input list 6, 4, 1, 2, 8, 3, 9, 5. Each black horizontal line in the illustration stands for a particular element in the list, and each coloured arrow represents a comparison and a possible exchange between elements. If the element at the head of the arrow is found to be less than the element at the tail, the two are swapped; if not, the order of the pair is left unchanged. You might like to check your understanding of this by tracing the operation of the procedure through the chain of lists produced by the successive comparisons and swaps.

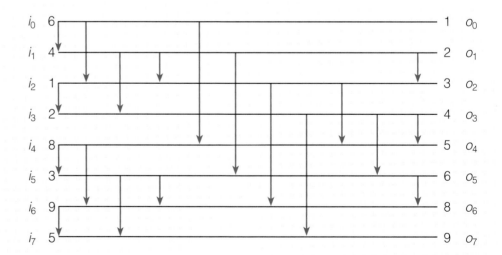

Figure 4.33   Batcher sort

Now, the big question is this: which is the network with the *smallest* number of swaps *guaranteed* to produce a sorted list at the end? For various reasons, networks operating on 16-element lists have been the most studied. The best procedure identified so far was discovered in 1969 and requires 60 exchanges. But there is a further, and more interesting question: rather than looking for networks by trial and error, could we program a computer to generate good networks for us and identify the best possible? As you are now well aware, this is a classic problem in *optimisation*. And as you know, optimisation problems are a major theme in computer science.

In 1991, Daniel Hillis took a radically new approach to this second question. Seeking to make use of the power of his Connection Machine, a massively parallel computer with 65 536 (2^{16} or 64k) processors, he wrote a program to *breed* efficient sorting networks by processes analogous to Darwinian selection. In Phase 1 of the experiment, the program searched the space of possible networks involving between 60 and 120 comparisons, using the following process:

1   Generate representations of 64k possible networks at random, and place one of these in the memory of each processor. At this point, we needn't go into great detail about exactly how a network was represented and why such a representation was chosen, as these issues will be covered in Block 5. It is enough to say here that each possible network was represented as 15 strings of 32 bits (0 or 1) each. Each string represented four comparison pairs, so, for instance, the sequence of bits:

    0111 1001

    represents the operation 'compare item 7 (binary 0111) with item 9 (binary 1001) – and swap if necessary'. For technical reasons, each comparison was coded twice.

2   The quality of each network could be judged by its ability to sort a set of test lists. Give each network a score based on these tests.

3   Destroy those networks that scored under 50%.

4   Pair up the remaining networks and exchange substrings of bits between the two members of each pair (again, we will cover the details of this process in Block 5), generating in each case a new network.

5   Change one or two bits at random in some randomly chosen strings.

6   There is now a new set of network representations produced by steps 4 and 5. Go back to 2 and start again with this new set of representations. Stop after a pre-decided number of repetitions.

Phase 1 of the experiment produced some respectable results. Many of the networks left at the end of the process were indeed efficient sorters, but overall the outcome was a bit disappointing. The problem seemed to be that the sorting networks evolved were good at sorting the test cases but performed less well on brand new tests. The judging process simply wasn't stiff enough. In Phase 2, Hillis came up with an inspired idea. He subjected the *tests* to the same pairing and culling process as the networks, but with the fitness of the tests being judged on their ability to resist being sorted: the best tests were the ones that proved hardest to sort, and it was only these successful tests that were paired up to produce the tests to be used in the next cycle. The results of Phase 2 were excellent: a sorting network requiring only 61 comparisons emerged – close to the best known.

Exercise 4.8

Look back quickly over this case study and try to relate it to what you know about evolution. Are there similarities between the procedures we described and natural, evolutionary processes?

Discussion

I hope you were able to detect some of the Darwinian themes here. The pairing up and exchanges between representations look a bit like *mating*. The random changing of bits has a similar effect to *mutation*. And the brutal culling process based on the success or failure of each network at sorting rather resembles *natural selection*. If you have any more specialised biological knowledge, you might also have seen in the evolution of the test cases a suggestion of the way animals and their parasites change together. As a creature evolves to be stronger and more resistant to its parasites, so new variants of the parasite are selected that are stronger and better adapted to attacking their hosts. The two are locked in a constant struggle.

There is no need to pretend that Hillis's experiment was in any way an exact replica of what takes place in nature. Natural evolution is obviously a much more complex affair, with many species simultaneously competing among themselves for mates, food and other resources, as well as with other species. But the analogy with evolution is clearly there. Nor do the processes we described depend on having a massively parallel computer. Exactly the same algorithm could be carried out by a conventional computer.

Roboticists, as well as computer scientists, now use principles of Darwinian natural selection as a form of adaptation, duplicating millions of years of evolution inside the computer to create behavioural architectures for their creations. Let's look at a single brief example, considering what changes as a result of this process.

Chocron and Bidaud (1999) of the Laboratoire de Robotique de Paris have described experiments in which an entire robot and its control system can be evolved from scratch. Using an evolutionary technique similar to the one you saw in Hillis' experiments, they can produce optimal robot designs for a number of different terrains. In these experiments, a robot can be constructed by putting together a number of modules of three main types: *segments*, *wheels* and *joints*. The purpose of the joints is to connect segments and wheels together in certain patterns. So an entire robot design can be expressed as a matrix, as in Figure 4.34. The number N_{sj} expresses the type of connection between a segment or a wheel S and a joint J. The control system can be expressed in a similar manner.

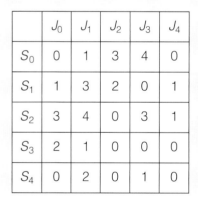

	J_0	J_1	J_2	J_3	J_4
S_0	0	1	3	4	0
S_1	1	3	2	0	1
S_2	3	4	0	3	1
S_3	2	1	0	0	0
S_4	0	2	0	1	0

Figure 4.34   Modular design matrix

Chocron and Bidaud used the following algorithm:

1   Generate a random set of modular designs and control systems, representing each as a matrix.

2   Simulate each of the designs and controllers on a computer and assess from this how efficient they are.

3   Destroy the ones that are no good.

4   Exchange information between the remaining design and control representations, producing a new one on each exchange.

5   Make small random changes to some of the representations.

6   Return to 2.

7   Stop after a certain time.

You can see that this is basically identical to Hillis's approach. By the end, only efficient and robust robot designs, with suitable controllers, are left.

Let's now move towards the end of this unit and the conclusion of Block 3.

4 Coda: Artificial life? Living computers?

This block has been concerned with the upsurge in interest among computer scientists in the properties of living things, and the lessons that computational models of living systems have for computer science and artificial intelligence. We've looked at the properties and the uses of a whole range of such models. But do you remember the questions about Vaucanson's Duck that came up in Block 1? What does the simulacrum teach us about the real duck? What does the model tell us about life? Could the model in some way approach the reality? A new and very active field of research in computing is **artificial life**.

On the other hand, can we turn these questions round the other way? If silicon-based computer systems tell us about life, or can even be seen as being in some way living themselves, might it be possible to set up carbon-based, living systems that are capable of doing *computing*? This is already being investigated, in the research field known as **molecular computing**.

A proper discussion of these two will have to wait until Block 6. For now, though, let me say a few words about these two pursuits.

4.1 What is artificial life?

Artificial life (or A-Life) is a term used to refer to attempts to create systems with some of the properties of living organisms. A-Life in its modern form was pioneered by Christopher Langton, who defined it as 'the study of man-made systems that exhibit behaviours characteristic of natural living systems'. I looked at some of these properties and behaviours in Unit 1; and while I decided there that it is probably as futile to look for some comprehensive definition of 'life' as it is to look for a comprehensive definition of 'intelligence', we can agree that among life's defining features are:

► self-reproduction;

► storage of a representation of the self, for the purposes of reproduction (think of genes and DNA);

► metabolism: that is, the ability of an organism to maintain a stable internal state, and to grow, by taking in and assimilating energy and new material from its environment;

► the ability to adapt, grow and evolve;

► autonomous interactions with the environment.

In Unit 1, I suggested that life may best be considered as a *continuum*: from crystals through to complex primates, taking in on the way doubtfully alive molecular systems such as viruses.

Given that living systems can be understood in terms of the way they process information and energy, how they behave, and so on, rather than by specific chemistries or structures, it follows that an entity might be recognised as living regardless of the substance it happened to be made of. Provided a system reproduces, handles energy and information, evolves, and so on, in appropriate ways, then maybe it has a claim to be called 'living' (although few, if any, artificial intelligence researchers would claim to have created anything living). Another way of looking at it is to focus on the behaviour of the artificial system. An artificial system might reasonably be called 'living' if its internal functions and its behaviour in the world are like those of living things. This leads to the possibility of artificial life.

4.2 DNA and molecular computing

You have seen that silicon-based biology has led to numerous computer applications and new advances in artificial intelligence. Carbon-based biology may also have a role to play in computing. Future generations of computers may not be based on silicon at all, but on complex biological molecules, such as DNA. Although still in their infancy, **DNA computers** can potentially store billions of times more data than a conventional computer, and solve difficult problems of exactly the kind we've been considering in the last two blocks.

We will return to both these subjects in Block 6.

5 Summary of Unit 4

This has been another long and detailed unit. In it, I've discussed some of the ways in which modern computer scientists are harnessing the principles of interaction, emergence, adaptation and selection in new kinds of computer systems, particularly robotics.

In modern reactive robotics, sophisticated robot behaviour can be made to emerge from interactions between simple behaviours within a robot, and between a robot and objects in its environment. I outlined two classic reactive architectures: Rodney Brooks's subsumption architecture and potential fields systems. You also saw an alternative approach in Beer et al.'s walking robots.

However, since all modern roboticists acknowledge that truly intelligent and practical robots have to be *adaptive*, I presented a brief and rather panoramic survey, with examples, of some of the ways in which flexibility, learning and adaptation are being built into the latest robots.

The unit ended with some blue-sky speculation about future computational systems that may lie right on the boundary between machines and living things.

Conclusion to Block 3

Block 3 conclusion

This block has tried to cover an immense amount of ground, and for that reason my coverage has necessarily had to be rather superficial. The time has come to narrow our focus and probe more deeply. In the next two blocks you will make a much more exhaustive study of two biologically inspired approaches to artificial intelligence and to computation, both of which have been foreshadowed here – neural networks and evolutionary computing.

For now, though, look back at the learning outcomes for this unit and check these against what you think you can now do. Return to any section of the unit if you need to.

You will find further case studies, exercises, links and other supplementary material for this block on the course DVD and the course website.

References and further reading

Further reading

In writing this text I've used over 300 sources. The list that follows is a selection of the sources that I consider you may find helpful in reading further on this topic.

Arkin, R. C. (1998) *Behaviour-Based Robotics*, Cambridge MA, MIT Press.

Bonabeau, E., Dorigo, M. and Theraulaz, G. (1999) *Swarm Intelligence: From natural to artificial systems*, New York, Oxford University Press.

Brooks, R. A. (1999) *Cambrian Intelligence: The early history of the new AI*, Cambridge MA, MIT Press.

Forbes, N. (2004) *Imitation of Life: How biology is inspiring computing*, Cambridge MA, MIT Press.

Griffin, D. R. (2001) *Animal Minds: Beyond cognition to consciousness*, Chicago, University of Chicago Press.

Murphy, R. R. (2000) *Introduction to AI Robotics*, Cambridge MA, MIT Press.

Sipper, M. (2002) *Machine Nature: The coming of bio-inspired computing*, Cambridge MA, MIT Press.

References

Bedau, M. A. (1997) 'Weak emergence', in Tomberlin, J. (ed.) *Philosophical Perspectives: Mind, causation and world*, pp. 499–508, Cambridge MA, MIT Press.

Beer, R. D., Quinn, R. D., Chiel, H. J. and Ritzmann, R. E. (1997) 'Biologically inspired approaches to robotics: What we can learn from insects', *Communications of the ACM*, vol. 40, no. 3, pp. 499–508, Cambridge MA, MIT Press.

Breazeal, C. (2005) 'Socially intelligent robots', *Interactions*, vol. 12, No. 2, pp. 19–22, New York, ACM Press.

Cordon, O., de Viana, I. F., Herrera, F. (2002) 'Analysis of the best-worst ant system and its variants on the QAP', *Ant Algorithms: Third International Workshop, ANTS 2002, Brussels, Belgium*, Heidelberg, Springer Berlin.

Chocron, O. and Bidaut, P. (1999) 'Evolutionary algorithm from global design of locomotion systems', *Proceedings of the 1999 IEEE/RS International Conference on Intelligent Robots and Systems,* pp. 1573–1578.

Clark, A. (1997) *Being There: Putting brain, body and world together again*, Cambridge MA, MIT Press.

Darwin, C. (1859) *On the Origin of Species by Means of Natural Selection, or The Preservation of Favoured Races in the Struggle for Life*, London, Dent (1928).

Deneubourg, J. L., Aron, S., Goss, S. and Pasteels, J. M. (1990). 'The self-organizing exploratory pattern of the Argentine ant', *Journal of Insect Behavior*, vol. 3, pp. 159–168.

Di Caro, G and Dorigo, M. (1998) 'AntNet: Distributed stigmergic control for communications networks', *Journal of Artificial Intelligence Research*, vol. 9, pp. 317–365.

Englebrecht, A. P. (2002) *Computational Intelligence: An introduction*, New York, Wiley.

Hillis, W. D. (1991). 'Co-evolving parasites improve simulated evolution as an optimization procedure', in Langton, C., Taylor, C., Farmer, J. and Rasmussen, S. (eds) *Artificial Life II, SFI Studies in the Sciences of Complexity,* Vol. X, Boston, Addison-Wesley.

Morowitz, H. J. (2002) *The Emergence of Everything: How the world became complex*, Oxford, Oxford University Press.

Kube, C. R. and Bonabeau, E. (2000) 'Co-operative transport by ants and robots', *Robotics and Autonomous Systems*, vol. 30, pp. 85–101.

Lumer, E. and Faieta, B. (1994) 'Diversity and adaptation in populations of clustering ants', *Proceedings Third International Conference on Simulation of Adaptive Behavior: From Animals to Animat*, vol. 3, pp. 499–508, Cambridge MA, MIT Press.

Nicolescu, M. N. and Mataric, M. J. (2005) 'Task learning through imitation and human–robot interaction', in Dautenhahn, K. and Nehaniv, C. (eds), *Models and Mechanisms of Imitation and Social Learning in Robots, Humans and Animals*, Cambridge UK, Cambridge University Press.

Norman, D. (1988) *The Psychology of Everyday Things*, New York, Basic Books.

Paley, W. (1809 [1800]) *Natural Theology; or, Evidences of the Existence and Attributes of the Deity* at http://www.hti.umich.edu/cgi/p/pd-modeng/pd-modeng-idx?type=header&id=PaleyNatur (last accessed 17 November 2006).

Russell, R. A. (2004) 'Mobile robot learning by self-observation', *Autonomous Robots*, vol. 16, no. 1, pp. 81–93.

Schoonderwoerd, R., Holland, O., Bruten, J. and Rothkrantz, L. (1996) 'Ant-based load balancing in telecommunications networks', *Adaptive Behaviour*, vol. 5, pp. 169–207.

Acknowledgements

Grateful acknowledgement is made to the following sources for permission to reproduce material within this course text.

Figures

Figure 1.1: Photo © Bill Schmoker;

Figure 1.3: Martin Harvey/Alamy;

Figure 1.5: Clive Bromhall/Oxford Scientific Films;

Figure 1.6: Robert L. Jeanne, University of Wisconsin-Madison;

Figure 1.7: Christophe Ena/AP/Empics;

Figure 1.8: Mary Evans Picture Library;

Figure 2.4: Courtesy of the Field Robotics Center, Carnegie Mellon University;

Figure 2.5: Dr Jeremy Burgess/Science Photo Library;

Figure 2.8: Claude Nuridsany and Marie Perennou/Science Photo Library;

Figure 2.9(a): Andrew Darrington/Alamy;

Figure 2.9(b): Neil Hardwick/Alamy;

Figure 2.10: Mary Evans Picture Library;

Figure 3.15: C.R. Kube, www.cs.ualberta.ca/~kube;

Figure 4.1: Courtesy of NASA/JPL;

Figure 4.2: Joseph Ayers, Northeastern University;

Figure 4.3: Mary Evans Picture Library;

Figures 4.5 and 4.10: Courtesy of Rodney Brooks;

Figures 4.6 and 4.9: Adapted from Brooks, R. (1999) *Cambrian Intelligence: The early history of the new AI*, Cambridge MA, MIT Press;

Figures 4.23, 4.24 and 4.25: Beer, R.D. and Quinn, R.D. (1997) 'Biologically inspired approaches to robotics', *Communications of the ACM*, March 1997, vol. 40, no. 3. Copyright ACM Inc. Reproduced by permission;

Figure 4.26: Adapted from Russell, R.A. (2004) 'Mobile robot learning by self-observation', *Autonomous Robots*, vol. 16, no. 1, Kluwer Academic Publishers;

Figure 4.27: Courtesy of Adam Russell.

Cover image

Image used on the cover and elsewhere: Daniel H. Janzen.

Index for Block 3

A

ADAM 146–149, 153–154

adaptation 63

affordance 123, 141

AFSM 129

altricial species 65

ant colony metaheuristic 84

ant colony optimisation 75, 78

Ant Colony System 89

Ant System 86

anthropomorphism 18

artificial life 162

augmented finite state machines 129

autonomous robots 150, 162

B

Batcher sort 158

Beer, Randall 142, 144, 157

behaviour 121
　　conscious 122
　　goal-directed 18
　　reactive 121
　　reflexive 121

behaviourism 65

Best–Worst Ant System 92

bifurcations 59

biologically inspired computing 38

biomimetic systems 119–120

blinkers 58

blocks 58

Bonabeau 45

bottom-up organisation 25

Brooks, Rodney 125, 128

C

carbon chauvinism 34

cellular automata 57

Chiel, Hillel 141

classification 28

Clever Hans 30

communication 29

competence 124

conditioning 65
　　operant 65

construction algorithms 76

coordinated algorithms 107

D

Darwin, Charles 68–69

data mining 110

demon actions 83

Deneubourg 44

DNA computers 163

drives 27

E

eaters 58

EDEN 146–148, 154

embodiment 52

emergence 57

engineering 23

evolutionary computation 69

evolutionary computing 157

excitatory signal 142

F

fixed action patterns 121

fluent coupling 51

formalism 36

G

genetic algorithm 157

glider 58

glider guns 58

graph theory 78

H

heteropathic effects 59

heteropathic laws 59

heuristic term 86

homeopathic effects 59

human–robot interaction 150

I

implicit knowledge 37

imprinting 121

inhibitory signal 142

interaction 44

K

knowledge
　　implicit 37
　　non-propositional 36
　　propositional 36
　　tacit 37

knowledge elicitation 36

L

learning 29, 65

LEMUR robot 119

local search algorithms 76

Lorenz, Conrad 121

M

Max–Min Ant System 91

metachronal wave 54

microrule 106

migration 12

molecular computing 162

N

nanorobotics 75

nanotechnology 75

natural intelligence 26

natural selection 68

neurons 56

non-linear interaction 61

non-propositional knowledge 36

nouvelle AI 38

O

operant conditioning 65

optimisation problems 74–76, 78, 83–86, 92, 101, 104–105, 114

P
Paley, William 25

parameters 72

parsimony 51

particle swarm neighbourhoods 102

particle swarm optimisation (PSO) 101

peppered moths 66

perception–action cycle 122

perpendicular field 140

pheromones 44

plume tracking 20

potential fields methods 128, 133

precocial species 65

probabilistic 79

propositional knowledge 36

psychosocial compromise 103

Q
Quinn, Roger 141

R
radial field 140

Rank-Based Ant System 92

reactive robotics 116–117, 125–127, 133, 145, 164

recognition 27

recruitment 44

reductive 59

releasing stimulus 121

response 28

Reynolds, Craig 48

Ritzmann, Roy 141

S
Schoonderwoerd, Ruud 94, 96, 98

selection 66

self-organisation 47

SENSE–ACT cycle 125

SENSE–PLAN–ACT cycle 49

signal
    excitatory 142
    inhibitory 142

situatedness 52

social robotics 150

space of attributes 110

space of representation 111

stigmergy 52, 108

stochastic 79

strong emergence 60

subsumption 129

subsumption architecture 117, 128, 132–133, 139, 141

swarm robotics 75

T
tacit knowledge 37

tangential field 140

taxis 21

Tindbergen, Niko 121

top-down organisation 24

transition rule 83

V
variables 72

W
weak emergence 60